I Served on Bataan

WIDE WORLD

The ceremony at Washington. Six American Red Cross Army nurses who escaped from Bataan stand at attention as Mary Beard, American Red Cross Director of Nursing, tells of the nurses' heroism. The nurses, left to right, are: Lieutenants Florence MacDonald, Mary G. Lohr, Harriet G. Lee, Eunice Hatchitt, Dorothea Daley, and Juanita Redmond. Mrs. Franklin D. Roosevelt is between Lieutenant Redmond and Director Beard.

ESS ASSOCIATION, INC.

A priest celebrates Mass at the open-air chapel of Lourdes in an army hospi
on Bataan.

I SERVED ON BATAAN

by

Juanita Redmond

LIEUTENANT, A.N.C.

J. B. LIPPINCOTT COMPANY

Philadelphia and New York

1943

Printed in the United States of America

Second Impression

I wish to acknowledge extreme indebtedness to the Hospital Staff of Bataan Hospital No. 1, which privileged me to serve as one of its members, and inadequately express my gratitude to my Mother, whose painstaking guidance and encouragement through life made this book possible.

ILLUSTRATIONS

I Served on Bataan

I

PEACETIME NURSING IN THE Philippines was very much like nursing in the States. Modern equipment in the hospitals, hard work while on duty, and good times off duty; the regular routine, varied by cases of tropical diseases, insects, damp heat, and that special feeling of cohesion which, I suppose, you find among people working together at one job in outposts all over the world. But a newcomer can be very homesick.

Certainly I was.

When I reached Manila in September, 1940, I floated down the gangplank complete in chiffon dress and an enormous picture hat, all ready for the welcoming committee that greets every Army transport, and for the customary entertainment at the Army and Navy Club. It didn't help my morale to find that American women in Manila dress very simply; my elaborate costume was no more suitable than it would have been in a Maine fishing village. Manila is—or was—a modern and sophisticated city, but there are good reasons why chiffon dresses and sheer stockings don't belong—such as tropical heat and voracious ants. It is—or was—a colorful city, its wide new boulevards and narrow old streets crowded with varied types of people, from the obstinately snobbish Spaniard to the tawny-skinned Filipino with his shirt-tail flapping over his trousers. Many of the homes are built after the old Spanish model, their eyes closed against the public gaze, the living quarters in the second story; and in the native quarters there are little huts of nipa or bamboo. Against the background of tropical foliage and time-grayed seventeenth-century Spanish churches, the big bright government buildings and modern homes strike a brave, incongruous note. And in and out among the up-to-the-minute automobile traffic weave—or used to—the gayly painted, horse-drawn, two-wheeled *calesa* carts. The air is hot and sticky, but to the north rise the purple peaks of the Mariveles mountains, ruggedly beautiful, and right at one's feet is the great landlocked harbor with the ships and the little fishing boats perpetually coming and going.

At least, it was like that in September, 1940, and that is the way I like to remember it.

At the time, I thought that home was very, very far away. Which I was to think again, much later and under circumstances I couldn't have imagined then.

I did not stay in Manila but went right on to Fort Stotsenburg, where I had been assigned, and where (after an initial shock at finding the hospital a group of low, neat wooden buildings looking rather like a frail summer resort) I soon settled down happily. The surroundings were very different from the Army and Navy Hospital at Hot Springs, Arkansas, where had been stationed for three years, but I learne to love the Philippines, both the country an the people, as I had thought I would when made application to be sent there. The experi ence of working with tropical diseases was in tensely interesting. About ninety percent of th Filipinos are afflicted with ascaris, the medica term for worms, from eating contaminate foods, in spite of the government's years of un ceasing effort to remedy this condition. Dysen tery is common, also; and tuberculosis, the hu mid climate of the islands encouraging th rapid progress of that disease. When an enliste American soldier showed the first symptoms, h was sent home immediately. Once we had leper case, a Filipino. He was soon transferre to a leper colony, but we never forgot him, no the instinctive horror that mingled with ou pity. When, at the end of a year, I was trans ferred to Sternberg General Hospital, larger and more modern than Stotsenburg, and with the added attraction of being in Manila, I was sorry to go.

At six o'clock in the morning on December 8th (which was the afternoon of the day before, at home) everything in my wards at Sternberg was going smoothly, like a satisfactory piece of clockwork. The soldiers with malaria, dengue fever, dysentery, colds, were receiving the usual early morning attentions which, also as usual, some of them sleepily resented. In an hour my charts would be finished and I would be off duty. I was planning to get in perhaps eighteen holes of golf in the afternoon.

I had no premonition when the telephone bell rang. As a matter of fact, when Rosemary Hogan's voice informed me that Pearl Harbor had been attacked, I laughed.

"Thanks for trying to keep me awake," I said, "but that isn't very funny."

"I'm not being funny. It's true," Hogan said. And something in her voice made me believe her.

It's always hard to realize that the thing you've talked about for years, while you felt secure and comfortable, has actually happened. I don't suppose more than a handful of us who gathered in the familiar Army and Navy Club to gossip and discuss everything under the sun ever took seriously the possibility that our jaunty invitations to the Japanese to "come on and invade us and see what you get" would be accepted.

They had the news in the Receiving Ward; the newspapers confirmed it in huge headline streamers: PEARL HARBOR BOMBED.

When I got back to the ward, I found someone had turned on the radio and the patients were listening. They weren't sleepy any more.

It would only be a matter of hours before we would get it too.

After I was relieved from duty, I decided to go to the bank. I felt very realistic and sensible; I would cable home my savings—just in case the Japanese *should* take Manila. There were so many other sensible people that a regular bank-run was going on when I got there. In all the streets there were crowds—Chinese, Filipinos in American clothes, Filipinos with their shirt-tails out, Spaniards, Americans—I didn't see any Japanese—all milling around uncertainly, as if they weren't sure of what to do or where to go, gathering in little knots to talk and then separating, still uncertain.

Back at the hospital I met Captain Mauppin.

"Baguio has been bombed," he said. "The Japs are reported flying down toward Stotsenburg."

"Baguio . . ." I repeated blankly. That

lovely resort, cool and remote in the mountains; and Fort Stotsenburg, only about forty miles away from Manila.

"We're in for it, aren't we?" I said.

"Yes," he agreed gently, "I guess we are."

But at Nurses' Quarters, Rosemary Hogan and Eunice Hatchitt and I, who had made up a "nurses' trio" for almost two years, found ourselves still incredulous, still clinging to the thought that it would turn out to be "just an incident," even while we silently dug out our helmets and gas masks.

Being on night-duty, this was our only time to sleep. But we didn't, and in the afternoon, during a lecture on gas detection and treatment while planes (of whose identity we couldn't be sure) droned overhead, the news came that Clark Field had been bombed, with heavy losses both of planes and men.

Doctors and nurses were hurriedly selected, and left for front-line service; to those of us who remained, Colonel Carroll (now commanding the American Medical Center for the continent of Australia) said quietly, "Well, girls, we're at war. Each of us has a job to do. I'm sure you'll do yours well."

But none of us had the faintest realization of what the job would be. How could we?

It was a relief to go on duty.

The men in the wards behaved well. The blackout heightened the sense of tension and once in a while a lighted cigarette would flare up, but not for long and not often. There was a good deal of talking, and all to one purpose: they wanted to get back to duty.

"There'll be boys needing these beds more than we do," one soldier said somberly.

He was right. Very soon afterwards all the patients it was safe to move were evacuated.

Early in the evening we were notified that several hundred casualties were on their way from Stotsenburg and Clark Field. I ordered my corpsmen (enlisted men in the medical units whose duty is to assist doctors and nurses in caring for patients) to get the ward ready, but by one o'clock we were still waiting. Ordinarily it takes only an hour and a half from Stotsenburg to Manila.

Hogan and I walked out to the entrance of the hospital, thinking up good sound reasons why the ambulances were taking so long. Then we heard planes. We didn't know as much as we did later, but somehow we knew those weren't ours.

Two flares went up not far away, near Nichols Field. Those were fifth-columnist signals, giving the boundaries of the Field, but we didn't know that then, either.

The bombing began right away, the exploding bombs and the anti-aircraft guns and flames licking up against the night sky.

I said, "Come on. We'll be needed."

Base Hospital No. 1.

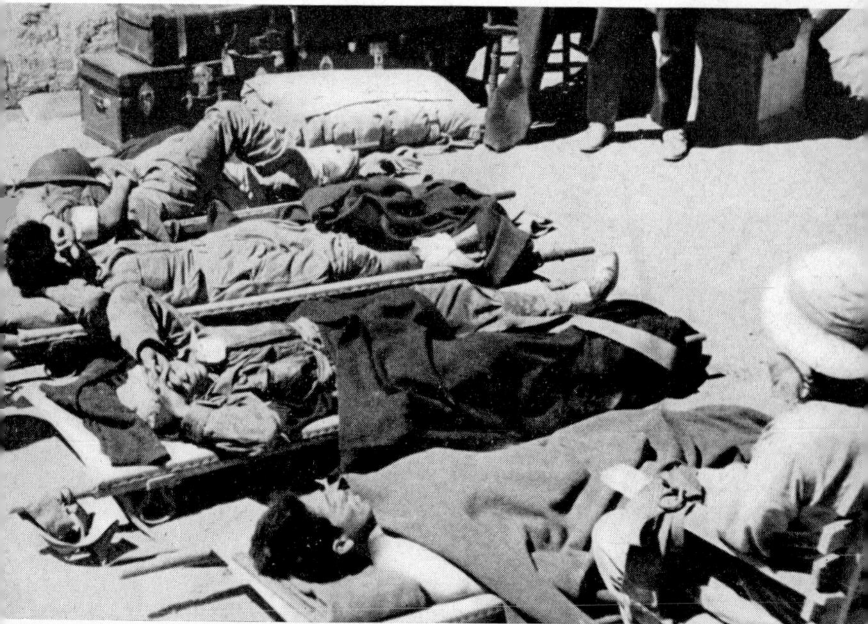

Casualties arriving in the receiving ward, Hospital No. 1.

Inside the hospital everybody was hurrying to assigned stations. We carried the patients too weak to help themselves out into the open where they would be safer if the hospital got a direct hit. Not only Nichols Field was being bombed, but the docks and Port Area, all the military objectives; and as we worked feverishly in the darkness the bombs came closer. We were naïve then; we didn't think of their *trying* to hit the hospital; still, it might happen by accident.

At about two o'clock the ambulances from Stotsenburg drove up, and at the same time the first casualties from Nichols Field began pouring in. All the nurses who could be spared were ordered to report to Surgery, I among them. The wounded came in trucks, ambulances, busses, carts, anything that had wheels. They were brought in on blood-crusted litters; many of them still bleeding, some with shrapnel lodged in their wounds, or arms dangling, or partially severed legs. And many were dead when they reached us.

Nurses and corpsmen stepped carefully among the litters that packed the surgery and the hall outside, giving shock treatment, removing blood-soaked clothing, making records, giving hypodermics. The operating tables were empty hardly a moment at a time.

The boys were so quiet.

They didn't scream or cry out. They clenched their teeth and fought the pain. Often and often one would insist, "Take my buddy, he's hurt worse than me."

I'll never forget my first war amputation.

We had got the soldier on the table and he tried to raise his head to look down at his leg.

"It's practically off, ain't it, Doc?"

"Yes, son."

"I guess it'll have to come all the way off?"

"I'm afraid so, son."

"Well, do a good job on it, Doc." And he grinned.

But they were all like that.

After eight and a half hours of that kind of thing, we were too tired to sleep. And the raids continued. Cavite, our naval base in Manila Bay, was bombed almost continuously that day. We couldn't stop watching the planes that seemed to blacken the sky, knowing most of them were Japanese, knowing that we had only a handful of our own to combat them.

But our planes brought down three of theirs that afternoon.

We watched the dogfight, about ten thousand feet in altitude, from which one Jap was knocked out, plunging straight into the bay. The pilots of the other enemy planes shot down were brought, dead, to the hospital. One was a German, a fact that was more interesting than surprising.

All the hospitals in Manila, military and civilian, were overflowing, and we were setting up new Army hospitals throughout the city, with the magnificent co-operation of Filipino doctors and nurses, many of whom went out, together with American doctors, to become part of the first-aid stations attached to each unit in the field, while others remained to staff the new hospitals. All available buildings—hotels, schools, public buildings, even the spectacular *jai-alai* palace—were turned into hospitals. Pharmacies and drug companies donated their supplies, and equipment was rushed from the U. S. Army Quartermaster.

We could see Cavite burning across the bay. Dark columns of smoke rose from oil tankers struck in the harbor. There were stories of native villages that had been completely destroyed; a few incendiary bombs landing on the dry nipa huts would set the whole *barrio* aflame almost quicker than it takes to tell it.

The roads to the hills were packed with refugees; the story of Poland, of France, Holland, Belgium was repeated. Only the setting was different; the human tragedy was the same.

It was hardly better in Manila. Everyone who could go fled to the hills, and those who stayed behind dug fox holes (any kind of ditch dug for shelter, whether a shallow pit or an elaborate affair with roof and sandbags, was called a fox hole) and cursed the planes as they passed over; and the look on people's faces was not fear but a taut, unyielding anger.

After the first bombings, the casualties were fewer; probably because the great majority of us acquired a deep respect for the potentialities of those sizzling missiles and would leap, without regard for dignity, into the nearest fox hole. Certainly in the hospitals we were grateful for the system of simple shelters dug outside the wards, the operating rooms, and living quarters, as we were to be later on in the jungle where the fox holes would be camouflaged with foliage and the limbs of trees.

Our trio had been separated, Hogan and Hatch remaining at Sternberg, while I was transferred to the new hospital in the *jai-alai* palace, where we used the huge courts for our wards. Others of our general group were scattered among the improvised hospitals in the city. It was not the easiest time to be deprived of old and tried friends.

Every day brought forth a new crop of rumors, each worse than the other. At that, the imagination couldn't think up anything much worse than the facts.

The radio informed us that eighty Japanese transports were entering Lingayen Gulf. A battle was taking place, with several transports successfully bombed, but nevertheless a landing was made in force.

We hadn't enough planes.

Japanese troops were marching on Manila

The American and Filipino soldiers, fighting superbly, were forced to withdraw.

The cavalry had been cut off.

General MacArthur had given the order to retreat to Bataan.

Rumor and fact—it was hard to tell where one began and the other left off. But we could all count the days until a convoy might be due; we could speculate endlessly (in our scant spare moments) when help would come. It didn't occur to us then to say, "*If* help will come."

II

ON THE TWENTY-THIRD OF DEcember a number of doctors, nurses, and corpsmen were ordered to Bataan. We were to be ready to leave early next morning from the *jai-alai* hospital, where the members of the corps from other Army hospitals would assemble, among them, to my joy, Rosemary Hogan and another old friend, Inez MacDonald. We were allowed one bag apiece, and as we had only the vaguest idea of what conditions we would find on the Peninsula, conferences and arguments about what to take along and what to leave behind were numerous and protracted.

However, at five-thirty in the morning we lined up in good order, most of us with a few white uniforms, a couple of pairs of white duty shoes, slacks, cotton stockings, undercloth-ing, cosmetics, and a very few precious posses-sions like photographs, as our entire personal equipment.

Ordinarily doctors, nurses and corpsmen would have been transported separately, but times had changed. A number of each group traveled together; if some of us didn't get through, the others could still set up a medical detachment. The busses—twelve of them, with two long seats running the length of the chas-sis, a railing down the middle to hang on by, and open sides—left at ten-minute intervals, and the drivers had orders to keep widely spaced along the road; no use advertising that we were a convoy or giving the Japs a chance to do a wholesale job of destruction on us.

Outside of Manila we made fairly good time, sometimes coming up too close behind the bus ahead of us, sometimes slowed by a sorry little procession of natives trudging along the roads, carrying what they had been able to save from their bombed-out homes. The luckier had *calesa* carts, piled with household goods and a baby or two on top; even the ponies had baskets on their backs. They were all, men and women and children and ponies alike, tired and pitiful, yet often they shouted good wishes as we drove by, or fingers would be uplifted in the *V* for Victory sign. We passed through the wreckage of native villages where a few short weeks before the naked brown-skinned babies had played under banana and papaya trees and among the stilts that raised the thatched-roof nipa shacks from the ground. We crossed streams where the women had once gathered to scrub and paddle the family wash, and gossip and laugh in the sun. There were rice-paddies where the *taos*, the peasants, had worked knee-deep in water, and water-holes with carabao wallowing for the relief of their insufficient sweat glands (without these periodic soakings,

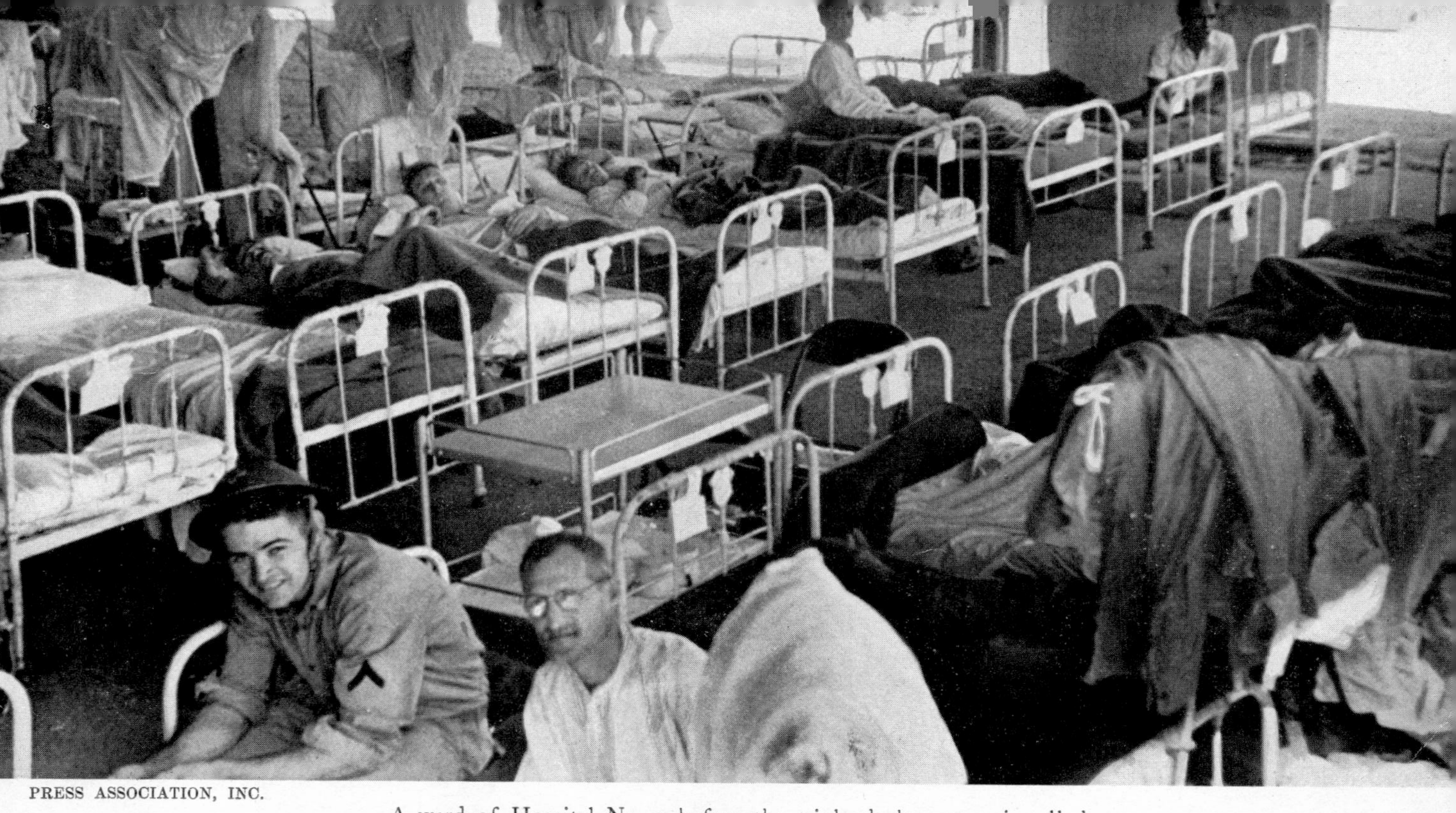

PRESS ASSOCIATION, INC.

A ward of Hospital No. 1 before the triple deckers were installed.

the great lumbering water buffaloes run amok), and we probably would not have believed him if some prophet had warned us that in the not distant future carabao would be the luxury item of our diet. . . .

Indeed, one of the boys was such a prophet, for at a *barrio* miraculously intact where we stopped to buy some bananas, he broke the food taboo by eating native-cooked wild rice.

One of the nurses said, "You're crazy. That stuff's contaminated or worm-infested or both."

"Listen, sister," said the soldier, chewing calmly, "you'll be eating worse than this before the party's over, and be damn glad to get it."

But we laughed at him. We felt very light-hearted. After the long strain of the past weeks, this trip was like going on a picnic. Even the planes that came over and sent us ducking into ditches along the road couldn't keep our spirits down very long. And soon after sundown, we thought, we would reach the hospital and find comfortable beds to roll into and sleep off the weariness of the hours of jolting stiff-backed travel.

The "hospital" at Limay turned out to be a series of depressed-looking wooden barracks, recently evacuated by the Twelfth Medical Regiment who had kindly left behind some of their personnel to show us the ropes. Nurses' Quarters consisted of a one-story wooden structure with a screened porch; inside were a lot of tiny rooms, with six beds scattered through them. There were fifty nurses in our group.

Someone said in a small tired voice, "Do we sleep on the floor?"

No, it seemed that in the storehouse—we were told with a vague wave of the hand, "Over there"—we would find beds and bedding. All we had to do was get them, carry them back, and assemble them. As the beds were in pieces—footboards, headboards, joining bars, and frames—this involved repeated trips back and forth. Then we returned for linens.

Still, it was peaceful that night on Bataan. No planes droned overhead, no guns thundered, no bombs fell. You could look up and see stars shining in the clear sky and smell the warm rich tropical earth untainted by explosives.

All of us, I think, forgot that the next day was Christmas. Perhaps fortunately. Our supplies had not arrived, and we had to create a workable hospital out of what seemed to us (spoiled as we were by all our previous experience in hospitals) impossible material or no material at all. We spent the day poking into corners, scrubbing and scouring, hunting through the storehouse for pots and pans and kitchen equipment; planning for wards and operating room; taking stock of the situation generally. The Twelfth Regiment continued to be our host for dinner, though one of our enterprising doctors proudly returned with a pig from a very small *barrio* near by, and about that time someone remembered—or felt it safe to mention—that this was Christmas Day.

Our celebration was not very hearty, I'm afraid.

Next day Colonel Duckworth, the Commanding Officer of Limay, gave me the job of setting up the operating room. Selecting two American and two Filipino nurses and several corpsmen as assistants, I opened the doors of the designated quarters—and found a bar-room, heavy with a smell of stale beer and littered with empty cans.

I felt like Hercules confronted with the task of cleaning the Augean stables in one day, only I had no convenient rivers to swish through the bar-room. We cleaned it, though, and when we got out our equipment and found we had been provided with adequate though not very modern instruments, which had been kept in good condition by a heavy coating of resin, we felt all the prideful joy of real accomplishment. To be sure, the walls were cracked, a grave defect in a supposedly sterile surgery, but optimistically we assured each other that this could be remedied, somehow.

Planes had been flying overhead all day, bombing nearby targets, and that evening we heard that General MacArthur had declared Manila an open city, that it was being stripped of anti-aircraft guns and other defenses. Supplies and equipment were being sent out of the city and the troops moved to Bataan and Corregidor. Doctors and nurses were moving the patients from all hospitals. We were routed out of bed that night to receive three hundred patients who had come in by boat. With them were many of our friends.

Nearly all the new Medical Corps arrivals were ordered to establish and staff Hospital No. 2, as soon as they found a suitable location.

After some intensive exploration, they decided on a site about five and a half miles from us and set up a large hospital there, under circumstances many times more difficult than ours had been. They had to start from scratch without even the forlorn barracks we had.

Meanwhile I was appointed dietician of our hospital. I took over a barracks for my kitchen, and for my chief cook I had Pop, who had been with the Army for twenty-eight or thirty years and was an excellent cook with the good chef's proverbial tendency to fly into tantrums.

He usually mumbled or grumbled when he spoke, as if afraid we might think him the least bit soft. Every part of Pop that we could see was tattooed, very colorfully, with flags and girls and ships and flowers and snakes, everything imaginable. The boys insisted that he was tattooed all over, and Pop would growl under his breath at that.

He had two assistants: Toby, a Mexican, and Blackie, an American soldier.

The kitchen had to be set up in working order in considerably less than a day, for with the influx of patients and medical units from Manila, we had not only some five hundred patients to feed that afternoon but the entire enlisted personnel as well. Later on, of course, the mess was broken down into several parts and our kitchen served the patients only.

Planning menus was easy enough, easier than it was ever to be again. The storehouse was rapidly filling up with the cases of supplies that trucks, carts and cars were still bringing out from Manila. There were fruit and vegetable juices, canned fruits and vegetables, tinned milk, rice and beans and flour; coffee and tea and cocoa. What luxury!

Pop could make tasty dishes out of practically nothing, but his specialty was corn fritters, and when word got around that corn fritters were cooking the mess hall would be stampeded. Pop's bark was worse than his bite. A little while after this, when supplies were beginning to run a bit short, Inez MacDonald had a birthday. Mac was pretty, good-natured and blonde, and a general favorite. Pop wanted to bake her a birthday cake, but a cake presented certain difficulties.

"How old is she?" Pop asked me.

"She might not like me to tell," I pointed out.

"Well, if we had candles, which we don't, how many would y'say to put on her cake, if she had one?"

"Oh, about sixteen," I said.

Later that day, one of Pop's assistants brought Mac a huge, delicately browned corn fritter. Stuck in it were sixteen burning matches.

Bombers came over us constantly, apparently trying for ships in the bay. It was pretty general practice to dive for fox holes when the alarm sounded. Pop, however, stayed in the kitchen. He had a theory, not original with him, that the bomb that would get him had to have "Pop" on it and when that one came along it wouldn't matter where he was. Nevertheless, he would stand in the window, yelling at the boys who stuck their heads out of the fox holes, "Get down, y' damn fools! Keep ya crazy heads down!"

Volunteers among the convalescents came to the mess hall every day to help make dressings and prepare supplies. Each one was given four cigarettes out of our scanty stock, as a reward; when that news got around, we had more volunteers than we could handle. The men talked freely as they worked, about their women and girls back home, but about the war too: When would there be a convoy? We don't need a convoy, we can do it ourselves. What about the blockade? Well, just suppose our fleet don't get through, what'll happen? Nuts, you could suppose night was day if you wanted to; there'll be a convoy, all right; and sometimes they told stories about the actual fighting they had seen, but not often, and usually the stories were roughly humorous; and they cursed the Japs for bombing defenseless Manila; but mostly they liked to show each other photographs and talk about home and home folks and good meals they had eaten and what they would like to eat right now. . . .

One youngster from Texas whose arm had been amputated worried a great deal about his girl. If he ever got home—that was the familiar phrase—they were going to be married. At least, that was what they had planned. Now, he didn't know. Maybe he shouldn't with only one arm. Maybe she wouldn't want him. At that point we would always hurry to tell him how proud the girl would be of him and of course they would get married, it would be

/ORLD

Result of a bombing raid on a Bataan village.

SOCIATION, INC.

What we saw from Limay.

plain foolishness not to. Only the other boys who had had amputations remained silent.

Rumors that we were to be moved back from the ever approaching ground-fighting began to run around the camp. At night, from our screened porch at Nurses' Quarters, we could see flashes of gunfire like heat lightning in the sky, and hear the tanks grinding by, the rumbling of trucks, and the tramp of marching troops not many yards away. Too frequently shells fell close to our flimsy wooden barracks with their thatched roofs, keeping us nervously strained with worry about the helpless men who were our responsibility.

There was one very bad night, and in the morning Colonel Duckworth ordered us to prepare for evacuation. It took us two days and two nights to move the patients. We used the *pambusco* busses that had brought us to Limay, and we did what we could to make the boys comfortable and safe. The seats were removed for the litters in which the badly wounded were carried; ambulatory splints replaced traction; the men in serious condition were given morphine. We worried about them as each load started out on the murderously rough jungle trail leading to Hospital No. 2. This hospital was taking them all, with most of our nurses as a supplementary staff. When the drivers came back for new loads, we would take time out to check up on our special cases. "Did Thomas make it?" we'd ask. "How was little Manuel, you know, the boy with the abdominal wound? And Bob Brown, and Stan, and Frederico . . . ?" So far as I know, not one of our boys died in this transfer. We were very proud and happy about that.

Then those of us who stayed behind packed up our few possessions in our battered bags and started out to set up a new hospital, further back in the jungle and high in the mountains.

We heard later that we had hardly gotten away before the empty Limay hospital was bombed; incendiaries had started fires, and all the barracks were leveled to the ground.

III

WE CALLED THE NEW LOCATION Little Baguio, because the climate was rather like that at the Baguio where we used to go from Manila to get away from the heat. The general set-up was very much like Limay, except that in addition to barracks and garages there were carabao stalls as well. Frances Nash had preceded us by a few days and already was started on getting her surgery in working order. We discovered two long sheds running parallel to one another, with no floors and open sides, but with tin roofs, and because of their size we decided to make these our wards.

I was still in charge of the mess and found, somewhat to my dismay, that the old one had been merely a rough small clearing in the jungle; I expected snakes to come out of the brush surrounding it. Kitchen supplies and utensils had been dumped in the middle, all mixed up with sacks of rice and cartons of canned goods. The stove was the crudest sort of affair, placed over a hole where the wood was supposed to burn.

Worst of all was the meat block. Evidently some of the men who had prepared their food there had left a chunk of carabao on the block. I couldn't see the meat; it was a solid mass of green flies.

I used a small garage shed for my kitchen, with a sort of out-door picnic arrangement for mess hall, with tables outside. It may sound very attractive, but there were difficulties. Little Baguio was cool for the Philippines, but the sun was as tropical there as anywhere else in the Islands, and sometimes it would be too much for the convalescent patients who, later, came to the tables. Then there was dust. It would blow up in the wind and settle on the food and in the boys' mouths and nostrils. But there wasn't any better arrangement we could make. No roofed sheds remained unused, and there was too little building material on hand to do any good.

We weren't long without patients. So many began coming in as the fighting on the Peninsula grew steadily more intense that I was called to duty in the wards, turning over the mess to one of the girls whom I had trained.

On night duty we worked without lights, though we had electricity of a sort. There was a long cord with a bulb at the end in each of the sheds which could be extended to any part of the ward. Most of the patients were brought in at night, for the Japs seemed to be making special efforts to bomb trucks, cars, and ambulances off the roads in the daytime.

The litter-bearers would come in a procession from Surgery, and I would turn on my flashlight to guide them to the unoccupied beds. Then a record was made from the field tag attached to the patient's clothing at the first-aid station. The tag gave his name, serial number, rank, organization, and possibly the diagnosis; after that the corpsmen got the patient undressed and I made him as comfortable as I could. The boys were very quiet, grateful for the comfort of a bed. They didn't complain about their wounds, but they wanted food.

"Please, mum, couldn't I have something to eat?"

"Can't you wait till breakfast? It won't be long."

"I'm so hungry. I haven't had anything to eat for days."

"For days? Wasn't there any food in your unit?"

"We were cut off. They couldn't get food to us."

It was a dialogue that grew more distressing

with repetition, and especially after our own food supply dwindled to near nothing.

One heavy night I went out to Receiving and Surgery to see if I could help. There were litters all over the ground outside. I leaned over one of them.

"How are you feeling? We'll be with you soon."

But there wasn't any answer. I thought perhaps he was sleeping, and I turned to another.

"Where are you hurt, Soldier?" and I picked up his wrist. There was no pulse. I turned my flash over the other litters. Their occupants were all dead.

Many of the men who arrived very far gone were saved by blood transfusions. We used blood plasma until our supply gave out; then we were all typed, and the doctors and corpsmen gave blood donations when it was necessary, but the nurses, at least in our corps, were never called upon.

We had a Japanese prison ward.

One day I was assisting at Surgery when a Japanese soldier was brought in with a broken arm which had been badly set and was now causing complications. The doctors had decided to break and reset it. The instant the anesthetist started to put him to sleep, he jumped off the table and raced all around the room before someone collared him. The Philippine-born interpreter said, with a touch of scorn, that he was shrieking:

"Don't kill me. Please don't kill me!"

We tried to make him understand that we weren't doing anything of the kind, only trying to spare him pain, but he kept on crying until the anesthetic took effect. When he returned to consciousness no interpreter was needed. He was the most surprised Jap I ever saw. He seized our hands and hissed and jabbered his gratitude and amazement; it was pitiful, and somehow embarrassing.

We asked him some questions through the interpreter, and he said all Japanese soldiers had been told by their officers that the Americans gave no quarter, took no prisoners, but would destroy them all, so it was better to die fighting.

"Why are you fighting?" we asked.

He looked astonished. "Because we are told to," he said.

But when we asked whether Americans could expect from the Japanese the same kind of treatment we had given him, he refused to answer.

The enlisted men took charge of the prison ward, but the nurses helped out whenever they could, though I am afraid curiosity had more to do with it than any spirit of sweet charity. Most of the prisoners were very young boys, and like our own boys they talked about going home after the war. A good many spoke English and knew all about the popular Hollywood actresses, giving expressive mmmm-s after each name.

When they were well enough they were sent to a concentration camp. A story circulated that one day the count of prisoners was sixteen and though none were officially admitted during that day, yet next morning the count came to twenty, a few deserters having wriggled their way in. Apparently, whether in the hospital or the internment center, the majority seemed grateful for decent treatment and were fairly well content. When planes flew overhead they always hoped out loud that they were American; most of us felt that this was less an attempt to curry favor than a perfectly natural dislike of being peppered with shrapnel, even Japanese shrapnel.

One day a Filipino was brought in with bullet wounds in the leg and arm. Sometimes pain creates a sort of false stimulation but in

Segundo's case his excitement was born of jubilation.

"I killed fourteen Japs this morning," he announced proudly. "I am very happy."

"Swell," I said. "A few more like you and the war will be over in no time."

"And one of them," he continued impressively, "is woman. Jap woman."

"A woman!" I exclaimed. "What was she doing?"

"She was behind machine gun. She was fighting. I slipped behind gun. She threw up her hands and say please do not kill me, I am woman." He waved his good hand. "She had pretty face, long hair. I hated to kill her. But she kill me if she can. She kill our people."

We had heard no reports of any women landing with the Japanese; possibly Segundo's victim had lived in the Islands and joined her countrymen when they invaded.

There were other reports about women, however; there were the dead Filipinas left in fox holes by the Japanese.

The Filipino soldiers, and especially the Scouts, were splendid fighters, very brave and very angry. Once I thought we were going to be unable to get an injured Scout into the hospital. He pushed us off, insisting that he had to keep on fighting, his friend had been shot and knifed and then hung to a tree after he was dead; he couldn't stop for his wounds to heal.

"We'll fix you up," one of the doctors told him grimly, "so that you can really do a job."

We had no trouble with him after that.

Another of our Filipinos told how he shot the gun out of the hand of a sniper who had tied himself into a tree. The Jap would not surrender, and the Filipino watched for eight days until his prisoner fell exhausted to the ground. It was hard to know how many or how much to believe of innumerable stories like this; frequently the very ones we said loudly we really couldn't swallow turned out to be true!

We spent our spare time—and very little of it there was—setting up a war-trophy table. There was a pair of rubber-rimmed spectacles from a dead Japanese; a food kit with hard-tack, tea balls, dried fish, and a little container of rice; a well-equipped medical kit, and an individual water filter. We had a collection of quite beautiful sabers taken from Japanese officers, and helmets and watches and buddhas, a loose suit of netting through which the Japanese wove foliage for camouflage, a Japanese flag, and the diary of a Japanese soldier. The convalescents loved to stand around the table admiring the trophies and exchanging tall stories.

In this hospital there were no kind friends and affectionate relatives to bring patients books and games and amusement. They had to make their own entertainment. We saved cardboard for them, which they cut up into playing cards or jigsaw puzzles. Somehow our chaplains, Protestant and Catholic, had managed to save some magazines, and these were very thoroughly read and passed along from one bed to another. The Filipinos spent a good deal of their time carving decorative pipes and cigarette holders from bamboo. Some of the things they made were quite beautiful, and the cigarette holder with carved flowers which a wounded Scout made for me is a cherished possession. Often after they were dismissed from the hospital they would send back to the nurses gifts of carved vases filled with flowers. The flowers were likely to be the wild orchids that grew in such profusion in the jungles as to be no novelty to us at all. What touched us was the trouble the boys took to give us pleasure.

There was a volley-ball field where the men of the hospital personnel played energetic games, often with teams from near-by camps, and a badminton court. They had rigged up an ingenious mechanical shower bath at the swimming pool and took showers with their helmets on. The helmets were some slight concession to the enemy planes. When they could find nothing else to amuse them, the men spent hours composing ribald songs deriding the Japs, or putting up signs such as "Free shaves for Japs, not responsible for mistakes," or playing jokes on each other which, I suppose, were not nearly so funny as we found them at the time.

Battles raged, and we were constantly adding new wards to the hospital. Originally set up to accommodate five hundred, at one time we had sixteen hundred patients to care for. Filipino workmen were brought in from the surrounding countryside to build bamboo beds, and both these and the regulation white-iron beds were double- and even triple-decked, except in the Orthopedic section. We were forced to spread out onto the strip of ground between the two tin-roofed sheds, and eventually cleared a patch of ground under some tall trees. There were no more bed frames, and mattresses were spread on the ground. Not that there were enough mattresses; blankets laid over the springs served in many cases. Some beds didn't have springs; others lacked pillows or pillow cases or sheets.

We were so short of linen we could hardly wait for one lot to dry before using it again, and often when we took the sheets from the lines run through the jungle it was difficult to tell that they had actually been scrubbed.

Then, dust blew through the sheds in clouds; we had to make rounds continually to brush the grime from the beds. Burlap draped from post to post helped a little. The latrine was another constant source of annoyance, unhappily one we could never forget for we had no lime and it was very offensive. Because of our dysentery patients who had to make as many as fifty visits to the latrine in a day, it could not be placed very far from the wards.

Yet with all our difficulties we had a smoothly-running, big hospital in operation. There was the Orthopedic ward, near my own General Medical and Surgery ward at the bottom of the slope; I could look up the hill and identify the patients by their "hung" extremities; for instance, the two arms protruding in the air marked the bed of José, and elsewhere an arm, a leg, both arms, both legs, sometimes both legs and both arms hung suspended in traction. I could watch Lieutenant Nelson peering through the little window of a plaster cast. The Orthopedic ward contained our X-ray equipment, in charge of Major Edward J. Kallus, and beyond the ward sheds, in what had been a garage, were the laboratory and pharmacy, where the personnel worked all night and all day, under the supervision of Lieutenant Perlman.

In the Surgery ward, just across from Orthopedic, I might see Hogan clambering up a crude ladder to reach a patient on top of a three-decker, and in the slope beyond I could watch Colonel Schock and Lieutenant Chamberlain in the Head ward (eyes, ears, nose and throat) examining a boy for whom they had molded a new chin. To the left, in Abdominal, Mac gave a patient an injection of glucose solution and the ward surgeon, Captain Charles Keltz, bent over a patient who had had an abdomen full of shrapnel while the wounded man moaned softly, beating his hand against the bed.

At one time or another all the doctors did surgery; the operating room was always functioning, even on those days when few new patients arrived. In the workroom that was part of Surgery, the nurses did such jobs as repairing rubber gloves and sterilizing the dressings that were prepared every day as part of the hospital routine. The dental clinic, near by, was almost equally active.

There were two wards devoted to general medical and surgery cases, and Lieutenant August Laudicina, a surgeon, would come into mine, cheerfully rolling up his sleeves and joking with the patients. As we went from bed to bed, he sniffed carefully, on the alert for gas gangrene cases, most easily detectable by their odor. He found a case of it on the morning I am remembering. The boy's leg had not only begun to give off the repugnant stench but was considerably puffed up.

"Chart," Lieutenant Laudicina said unhappily.

The soldier's records showed that he had been left on the field some time before he could be brought to the hospital.

When the litter-bearers came to carry the patient out to the open-air gas gangrene ward, there was a stir of concern all through the ward, and the boy lifted frightened eyes to the doctor.

"It gets worse all the time," he said.

"Colonel Adamo's treatment will fix you up," the doctor assured him, and as I remember it, it did.

Colonel Adamo's method was something we were all very proud of. Bataan's earth is heavily infected by anaerobic bacteria, the germ responsible for gangrene in wounds, and in the early days of the war the prevalence of gangrene complications was very serious. The supply of the serum which had been developed after World War I, and took the place of Dakin's solution, ran out and for a while experiments were made with the sulfa drugs, fairly successfully, until our supply of those was almost exhausted. Colonel Adamo's treatment was developed, like so many medical advances, under the stress of emergency, and has the great merit of simplicity and directness.

The wound is cut open, perhaps the entire leg laid open to the bone if it is that far gone, and the infected tissue removed. Then, after being swabbed with peroxide, the morbid area is left uncovered except for mosquito netting, while the exposure to sunrays and oxygen destroys the bacteria.

The gangrene ward, on a low hill away from the hospital sheds, was certainly not the pleasantest place in the hospital. The putrid odor, the ugly exposed wounds, the monstrous limbs where the infection had not yet been cut out, the agonized moans of "Take it off, please take it off," made it a place to avoid when one could.

Yet it is connected in my mind with an amusing incident—which is one of the things one learns about war; tragedy and humor, the things you want to forget and things you hope you'll remember, are all inextricably mixed up together. This was a night when a storm was blowing up, and I thought of the gangrene patients on the hill with no shelter over them. I had one end of the shed cleared out far enough away from the other patients not to contaminate them, and then we rounded up as many corpsmen as we could and began carrying the patients down from the hill. It had begun to rain in solid sheets, and we had to work in darkness; I followed the litter-bearers with a flashlight pointed to the ground to keep them from stumbling over rocks and roots of trees, and there was a ravine to be crossed into the bargain. We were doing pretty well, carrying the beds themselves rather than transferring the sick men to stretchers, when suddenly a man in one of the beds sat bolt upright.

"What in hell's going on here?" he shouted. The next instant he jumped out and started to run.

"Don't run, don't run," I called in an agony of anxiety. "Wait, we'll take you in."

I turned my flashlight on him, and recognized one of the corpsmen.

"*Well,*" I said furiously, "what in the name of Pete were you doing in that bed, Caston?"

Trying feebly to pull his shirt further down his bare legs the corpsman explained sheepishly that he had been so tired when he went off duty he didn't know quite where he was, and finding an empty bed he simply flopped on it and fell sound asleep.

"You get your trousers and help us move the other patients," I said in the sternest voice I could manage. Which he did, apparently so glad to have his trousers on safely that he didn't mind working while off duty.

IV

ONE OF OUR FAVORITE PATIENTS was Freeman, an American boy about eighteen years old; both his legs had been amputated above the knee. He was quiet and charming, and his fame had spread, for many soldiers passing by the camp would stop at the hospital and ask to see "that young fellow who's lost both his legs." I would nod towards his bed, which I had placed near my desk because he so seldom asked for attention that I wanted to keep him under my eye. Freeman would say brightly, "I'm fine. How are you?", and it was curious to watch the expression that crossed the strangers' faces as they tried to smile in reply.

Someone gave him a radio and we brought him books and cigarettes whenever we could. It never occurred to those of us who knew him well to pity him; we respected him too much.

A young Filipino named Eugenio was very dear to us too. Both of his eyes had had to be removed because of a severe head wound. At first he was terribly depressed and seldom spoke, though he made us see he was appreciative of everything we did, or could do, for him. Doctors, nurses, corpsmen, and the patients who could navigate under their own power, made much of him. Someone was always near his bed, reading to him or making conversation, and Eugenio's spirits improved rapidly. When he began to convalesce there was always someone with spare time to take him walking. He quickly grew remarkably keen of hearing, and he became a very familiar figure, picking his way slowly through the wards, a gentle questing look on his face. While we were working we would often feel a soft tapping on our shoulders, and know it was Eugenio, not wanting anything, but "seeing his way" about.

Our patients suffered not only from bullet and shrapnel wounds but from the malaria that was spreading throughout the Peninsula. Few deaths result from the ordinary type of malaria; the patient is left, after his cure, in a weakened condition, but quinine dosages, rest, and proper nourishment insure recovery.

And now we were having cases of a cerebral type of malaria that proved invariably to be fatal. Fortunately it was rare. The Filipinos were the only victims so far as we saw them, and they were usually admitted to the hospital in a convulsed, unconscious state. We could not give them medicine by mouth; quinine had to be given intravenously. Experimental treatments were tried, but nothing seemed to help.

The doctors were very much concerned about it, and took some sheets to screen off a section of the woods where they could perform autopsies and, perhaps, learn more about the disease. One of my Filipino patients, endowed with an outsize bump of curiosity, headed in the direction of these sheets, though he had been ordered to stay away. I saw him going, but it was too late to reach him. He thrust his head into the improvised morgue, and immediately bounced back, howling like a madman. I had to send a corpsman out to bring him back from the woods, and he was a very sick boy for the rest of the day.

Dysentery, beriberi, and other disorders due to malnutrition and impure water were on the increase. A typical case was a young American soldier suffering from a severe attack of diarrhea, who said that for the last several days he had had nothing to eat but a few bananas and those only because he had stumbled accidentally into a grove of banana trees.

"But I think it's really because of the water," he told us. "We were cut off from our base; our canteens were empty and we were dying of thirst. We saw this carabao stream. It was awfully dirty but we just had to drink. You get so thirsty you don't care what you gulp down your throat so long as it's wet."

There were stories of eating lizards and snakes, and of living for days on an exclusive diet of horse meat. In one unit where the men had been without food for days, the captain dismounted and shot his horse. They butchered it and used as much of the animal as they could, cooking it out in the open; but they were severely ill when they returned to camp.

We kept a watchful, and fearful, eye on our own food supplies. We had been down to a two-meal-a-day schedule since the Bataan siege began, no new replacements were being made, and none of us had illusions about the probable shrinkage of those meals, if help didn't reach us very soon. Many of us had begun to draw in our belts and everyone was hungry between times. Captain Fraley, the Quartermaster, looked perpetually worried. He was always going off somewhere to find food, usually by the barter method, though we had little left to barter. Fortunately for us as many carabao as could be rounded up had been driven to the Peninsula as soon as it was known that evacuation to Bataan was imperative, and often enough our two meals a day would consist of carabao stew.

Captain Charles Osburne was a likable, good-natured, slightly bald and rather fat man, whom we had teased about being overweight. In the afternoons when he returned from reconnaisance we always kept a lookout for him. We were eager for news of the front lines and sometimes we could get specific information from him, but he always tried to spare us.

"Captain Charlie, what's the word today?"

"Oh, it's very good," he would boom out in his jolly voice. "Very good today," even when he knew that we knew it wasn't anything of the kind.

Now we couldn't heckle him about his overweight; instead we teased him about getting thin. Then he'd pat his diminishing abdomen.

"You're right, girls," he'd say, "it looks as though I'd regain my boyish figure after all."

One morning Blackie, one of Pop's assistant cooks, came to me while I was gloomily eating what passed for breakfast.

"We're goin' to have a bang-up meal this afternoon," he confided. "Steaks!"

"No!" I exclaimed. "But that's a miracle. There isn't . . . there isn't a convoy in, Blackie? Or did Corregidor send something over?"

He shook his head mysteriously. "You'll see," he told me.

But when we sat down at the table in the afternoon and there actually *were* steaks, I suddenly wanted a better explanation.

"Blackie," I said sternly, "just what are these?"

He leaned over my shoulder. "Remember

that light horse you rode in Manila you're always talking about? Well, that might be part of him."

I pushed away my plate, feeling a little sick. But the others ate it and seemed to enjoy it. I thought of all the horses I had ever ridden, of polo ponies thundering across green turf, of good patient dray-horses, of hard-working pack horses and temperamental mules. Then I thought of the Army units who had had nothing but horse meat for days.

Then I stopped thinking, and ate. I didn't like it, but I was too hungry not to eat.

But poor Blackie was punished for his teasing. He went around the camp asking everyone anxiously:

"Anybody see my Tojo?"

Tojo was his pet monkey. We had several monkeys around the camp, all of them named Tojo after Japan's prime minister, and most of them first-class nuisances. Blackie made a thorough search of the camp, calling, "Tojo, Tojo, here, Tojo," coaxingly. Dark suspicions lodged themselves in his mind; you could almost see them gathering. Glowering, he investigated further in the jungle. His hunch was right. Several of the boys were enjoying monkey stew.

Someone said that pythons were very good eating, but unless Blackie had a change of heart and decided what I didn't know wouldn't hurt me, I don't think we ever ate python meat.

I think our feeling about help coming from home had gotten to be a constant, nagging, but almost unconscious thought in the back of our minds. Of course we talked about it; we talked about it a great deal. Every day the doctors, nurses, corpsmen, and patients made bets with each other as to how many hours, days, weeks —we didn't dare make it any longer than that —it would be before our boats reached us. The bets were often in the form of a case of beer or a case of Scotch, to be paid on our return to

Manila. And the men, and nurses too, would climb to the top branches of a tall tree on the hospital grounds, from which we could look out over the bay. If there were ships coming to our rescue we could see them from there. But I believe most of us were afraid to think about it alone with our own minds; and we were very busy, we were working harder than we ever had, we couldn't spare the strength to face the real possibility that help might never come.

A problem peculiar to the feminine personnel was keeping up appearances—*our* appearance. It's an axiom that a woman's morale goes up or down according to the way she looks, or thinks she looks. At Limay we had been lucky enough to have a Filipino civilian do our laundry, which he did very nicely, taking the greatest pains with our white uniforms. However, later on our clothes were left unpressed, and attached to each girl's bundle was a note:

"Dear mum, I am sorry to return your clothes no finish press but we cannot get charcoal. As we are at war, I know you will understand and will not mind wearing your clothes unpress from top to bottom. I am your faithful servant until the Japs come get me."

At Little Baguio we put aside such frivolities. We worked in coveralls, which were ugly and much too big for us, but very practical; our white shoes were white by courtesy only; what was left of our cosmetics was hoarded like a miser's gold, to be used only on the rare occasions when we "went to a party."

For there were party occasions of a sort, even then.

There was the evening when Major Montgomery and Lieutenant Wheeler drove us down to Mariveles in a jeep. Mariveles is a tiny port at the tip of the Peninsula and it had been thoroughly bombed. Under the bright moon the wreckage was sharply defined. The little homes, the shops, turned dead, gaping mouths to the sky. In the center of the square stood a statue, the only thing left unscathed, commemorating the first rebellion of the Filipinos against Spanish rule in 1896, and over one of the outstretched arms someone had tossed a wreath.

The same officers were responsible for a vastly more successful party, however. Eunice Hatchitt from Hospital No. 2 and I were invited to dinner at the motor transport battalion camp, where we had baked ham and fried ham, stuffed wild chicken, custard and coffee, complete with a menu, printed on a cardboard tacked to the trunk of the tree under which the table was set, and headed in large letters, WELCOME TO VICTORY HOTEL. Obviously Motor Pool No. 1 had been carrying on some fancy bartering with the natives, for they were no more immune from the food shortage than any other camp.

After dinner there was entertainment, with formal typewritten programs:

ENTERTAINMENT
Under the Auspices
of
THE VOICE OF CABCABEN

Somewhere in Bataan Mountain, Philippines

Master of Ceremonies: Corporal Fernandez

PROGRAMME

1. *Vocal Solo (In Tagalog) Mr. Agapito Bulan*
   (Serenaders of Aetas)
   Guitar Accompaniment... Mr. José Gerones
2. *Guitar Solo....... Corp. Fuastino Dadivas*
   (King of the Balugas)
3. *Vocal Solo (In Spanish) Sgt. Perfecto Pinion*
   (The Lost Mestizo)
4. *Vocal Duet............. By two ladies*
5. *Clarinet Solo....... Pvt. Gonzales, Tomás*
   (Shanghai Swingster Fragment)
6. *Solo.................... Miss Cabcaben*
7. *Vocal Duet....... Pvt. Salgado, Artemio*
   Mr. Agapito Bulan

8. *Hocos Bugos Magic . . . Sgt. Paciano Balabis*
9. *Guitar Solo . . . . Mr. José Gerones*
(Lost from Kongo)

Note: You are welcome. Tune in again sometimes when invited. May God bless and keep each one of you. Goodnight.

Epefanio Fernandez,
Master of Ceremonies.

ADDITIONAL ATTRACTION

Moro Moro Dance . . . . Pvt. Espiritu, Eduardo
(The lone reinforcement from Chungking)

Neither "Miss Cabcaben" nor the Moro dancer appeared, but this lack was compensated for by the fact that the guitarist, José Gerones, had just escaped from the Japs, after several weeks' imprisonment.

There was a good deal of friendly trading of foodstuffs between units, and extras (usually in the shape of pigs or chickens) were shared whenever it was possible. But our most generous source was the gunboat, *Canopus*, heir to supplies removed from Cavite before the village was bombed. The nurses had a standing invitation to dinner on board, and occasionally some of us managed to take advantage of it. Inez MacDonald and I went one day and were almost overcome by nostalgia at the sight of the silver and table linen. They gave us wonderful food and lots of cigarettes, and after dinner we played bridge with Captain Pohlman and Lieutenant Erickson. It was fun and relaxing. When the Chaplain said good night he handed us each a lollypop; we could hardly believe our eyes. The very word, "candy," belonged to a dead language.

It was hard to believe we were taking a chance in visiting the ship, but, though well camouflaged, it had been spotted by the Japanese, bombed and almost sunk. However, everyone was taking chances all the time, and we had adopted Pop's philosophy—"if it's gonna getcha, it's gonna getcha." You might as well have a good meal at the same time.

The cigarettes from the *Canopus'* supply were most precious of all. The hospital store was almost exhausted. Some of the Filipino soldiers would offer a peso (equivalent in the Philippines to about fifty cents) for one cigarette, and I have heard American soldiers say they would pay twenty U. S. dollars for a pack or one hundred and twenty dollars for a carton. But as long as we had them, they were generally shared on a purely friendly basis. Except for the barter system of course, which was friendly enough. When we still had canned peaches the doctors would exchange their share for the nurses' cigarettes. The nurses were luckier than anyone else in the matter of cigarettes, for visitors from better situated bases frequently brought them to us and the *Pigeon*, another Navy ship, often sent us a supply.

Lieutenant Laudecina used to come into the

ward and say, "Well, Red, how many cigarettes have you this morning?"

"Oh, I have a few."

"Just a few?"

"Well, Tom brought me some."

He would throw up his hands. "I know. There are two kinds of people in this world, the Haves and the Have-nots." That was my signal to hand him a pack.

It was hardest on the men in the combat forces. When the boys in the jungles couldn't get cigarettes they rolled up leaves and smoked them, and frequently were very sick. That didn't stop them, though they would be more careful afterwards of the leaves they chose. At daybreak you could see the civilian Filipino laborers going around the grounds with a tin can, collecting the very tiny butts, from which they painstakingly manufactured cigarettes for themselves.

There was always a great deal of coming and

going on the grounds between the sheds housing the wards, the Nurses' Quarters, the kitchens, the laboratory, the dental clinic, Surgery and Receiving. Nearly everything was open to view, and we could have few secrets from each other. We could watch our commanding officer, Colonel Duckworth, measuring out, with his adjutant, Captain Lamire, the space he knew by heart, trying all over again to find some way to expand the hospital. Edith Schacklett would be hurrying into one of the wards with some special delicacy concocted for a seriously sick boy, and then run back again to our little nurses' home which she kept comfortable for us in spite of unimaginable obstacles. And often from the wards we could see the two chaplains sitting calmly at the desks that also served as pulpits, reading their Bibles.

However, most of the time the chaplains were kept very busy. They visited among the boys, planned entertainments for them, gathered together soldiers from outside units to put on shows, read to the boys with eye injuries, distributed cigarettes when we had them, and of course conducted services. Several of the soldiers had built an altar, complete with a crucifix, for Father Cummins, and just across the way was Captain Frank T. Tiffany's Protestant chapel, encircled by a wire fence with native cane laced through the wires by some of the Filipinos. Each chapel had seats made of boards laid across wooden sawhorses and could seat about fifty people. The Filipinos fashioned communion cups out of bamboo, and vases for flowers. The vases were always filled for services, the boys saw to that.

And when we had little Bataana with us, every head turned and every foot that was able scurried in her direction as a nurse carried her, like a queen, from Surgery down to the Abdominal Ward. For we had a maternity case at Little Baguio.

The mother, a Chinese *mestiza*, or half-caste, had come to the jungle to be with her husband, an American soldier who had been in the Army for some time. He had received a foot injury and was in the hospital himself at the same time the baby was born. We fixed a place for the mother in the Abdominal Ward, screening her bed with a number of sheets, and until the birth was over, we seemed to have a whole ward of expectant fathers on our hands. Everything went well, the baby was pretty and blue-eyed and by far the most popular person at the base. We kept her in Surgery and brought her down to her mother at feeding-time, and all the doctors as well as the nurses clamored for the job of carrying her. The patients who could sat up to gaze at her and those who couldn't move demanded to see her, while wistful eyes and soft clucking noises followed her as she passed by.

She was promptly named "Bataana," but it

was not so easy to find a layette for her. Some of the nurses had twine bags which could be unraveled and made into sweaters and booties. Captain Fraley had one of the Filipino boys weave a pretty bassinet of rattan, and we even enlisted the aid of Corregidor in the matter of supplies for our baby.

When the mother took Bataana away to her quarters further in the jungle, the whole camp felt lonely and let-down. There is something very normal and reassuring about a baby; small Bataana's presence was like a pledge that some day life would be sane and sweet again.

The reports that came in from the outside world gave us no such assurance. The news we got over the radio from Headquarters in Corregidor and the mimeographed news dispatches gathered from shortwave broadcasts, written up at Headquarters and sent out by the inter-island boats which operated until the fall of Bataan—nearly all the news was bad.

Once our spirits soared sky-high. Convoys were on their way to Australia. Surely, surely, they would break through to us. . . . We hugged to ourselves each optimistic report: about the Russians, and the rising production at home; and the fighting anger of the English and their relief from the incessant bombing of the year before; we were avid for news from China, for China was fighting the enemy facing *us*, had been fighting him for many years, and our sense of kinship with that brave ally was very strong. When the report came that on February 23rd the Japanese had shelled Santa Barbara in California, some one cracked: "So MacArthur wired U. S. officials that if they can hold out for thirty days we'll send 'em help."

I suppose the leaflets dropped by Japanese planes come under the heading of "outside news." They were very fond of bombarding our lines with leaflets, most of which attempted to undermine the Filipinos' loyalty to America. One was especially obnoxious. In one corner there was a hideous caricature of President Roosevelt sneering at a dead Filipino who lay on bloodied ground near barbed wire. A pitiful Filipina kneeled beside him, weeping and holding an infant in her arms, while near by stood an older girl also weeping. Beneath was printed:

Roosevelt, the World Enemy No. 1

> We, the Japanese forces, pay its deepest homage to those who died or wounded on the battlefields. We pledge ourselves to make reprisal on our common enemy, America.

They were all about as subtle as that. A booklet carried a picture of a beautiful, practically nude Filipina on the cover; the caption assured you that she was waiting at home for her Filipino soldier who was risking his life in a war that wasn't his. On an inside page ballroom dancing and a spread feast was portrayed—the foods easily distinguishable and calculated to make a hungry soldier's mouth water. "Behind the line," the caption said, "the Filipinos are enjoying all the luxuries. Why not throw down your arms and join them?"

In other leaflets the Filipinos were urged to throw down their arms and surrender; they were promised safe conduct through the Japanese lines; they would be permitted to return safely to their homes; all courtesies would be accorded them.

On March 14th we heard that General MacArthur had left for Australia.

President Quezon had gone, too. General Wainwright was promoted and ordered to Corregidor. The changes increased the general feeling of tension, and there was a certain sense of confusion, mingled with satisfaction that General Wainwright, whom we all knew and loved and who had been a familiar figure on Bataan, was at Headquarters.

On the 18th the radio from Corregidor announced that the General's party had reached Australia, and at about the same time the Japs bombed us with cans. Literally, cans; decorated with the Japanese colors of red and white, and about the size of a tin of tomatoes. We thought at first they were some new kind of trick shell containing an explosive, but on investigation there seemed to be something inside that sounded like paper.

It turned out to be a letter, addressed to General Wainwright, and it began by praising the valiant stand of our Army. However, it continued, we were outnumbered and overwhelmed, and if the General did not surrender by March 22nd, we would be bombed fifteen days and nights consecutively and no mercy would be shown.

That "letter" from the Japanese was one of the very few letters to get through to us. When any did come in, by some means or other, they weren't regarded as purely personal property but as belonging to all of us, and were passed around for everyone to read.

So when, also during March, Edith Schacklett received a Christmas package we all stood around while she opened it, quite as excited as she was. The box had been sent from home before December 8th.

When the last fold of tissue paper had been lifted, there was a chorus of loud, incredulous sighs. Then someone laughed, and we all broke down into something perilously close to hysteria.

It was a hat. A pretty little, frivolous black hat, with a dainty veil.

Dressed in her none too clean and very much too large coveralls, with Government-issued men's shoes, that were too big also, on her feet, Shack twirled the hat tenderly around.

"It's awfully cute," she said wistfully.

She put it on, adjusting it with great care, and at the sight she made we collapsed again. But I think tears weren't too far under our laughter.

That hat! It symbolized home, and theaters, and dinner in soft-lighted restaurants, and city streets. People came from other camps just to look at it; you could see in their faces that they were wondering if they'd ever get back to a place where things like that weren't bitter incongruities.

The shortage of medical supplies was getting to be a serious problem. Our one P-40 plane would fly to the southern islands after nightfall and bring back supplies some hours later, but it could only carry small quantities of essentials.

There were many days when we were out of quinine. We were running short of dressings, and had to use them very sparingly. Some we removed carefully from the patients, washed them in boiling water, sterilized them, and applied them again.

At the beginning of the war an order came through requiring every person on Bataan—soldiers, doctors, nurses—to take ten grains of quinine a day, five grains in the morning and five at night. But when the real fighting began, units were cut off from their bases; supplies couldn't be renewed.

At the hospital we tried using plasmoschin and atabrine, except on the very sick patients.

Our P-40 kept us just short of disaster, and we were proud of it, but not only for that reason. In the earlier days on Bataan an improvised bomb-rack was built on the P-40, which went off to bomb a Japanese ship in the Gulf.

That night the Japanese broadcasted over their regular propaganda program that the Americans had sent forty-six planes to bomb their ships and the open city of Manila as well.

Our boys remarked grimly that if we'd really had forty-six planes there wouldn't have been a Japanese ship or plane left in the Islands.

V

WE HAD OUR FIRST RAID ON March 30th.

I went on duty at seven in the morning, and aside from the fact that it was rumored more Japanese transports had arrived, the day seemed like any other—until I heard the sharp whizzing of a bomb. It sounded closer than any I had heard before. The next one was nearer, and threw me to the floor, several of the patients with me.

It seemed to me the explosions went on forever, though actually it wasn't long. When the bombing stopped, I got up from my cringing position on the floor and saw flames shooting in every direction.

The wards had been missed, but several of

the other buildings, and cars and trucks, were burning.

I didn't go outside, for there was plenty to do in my own ward, but I could see everyone working wildly, throwing buckets of dirt on the fires, and the litter-bearers hurrying off into the jungle after casualties.

Settling the patients and taking care of the new-wounded kept me busy for a long time. When I could leave the ward, I didn't know whether I wanted to or not. There were sheeted figures on the ground, most of them hospital personnel, men we'd been working with a long time; men we knew and liked.

But, as raids go, we had been lucky. A bomb had landed near the doctors' nipa hut, taking half the house away. Another nearly struck the Surgery, shattering its few windows. The Receiving ward had a near-miss and shrapnel from this bomb had flown into our shed breaking a water cooler. At Nurses' Quarters our few possessions had been thrown off the boxes we had set up; the frames of photographs cracked and the glass entirely gone. But all the material damage could be repaired fairly quickly.

There was the usual post-bombing checking on friends, and comparing notes; we all told each other where we were when the bombs struck, what we thought and felt, the way people do after their first raid.

Our receiving set had been among the casualties, and we couldn't get the regular *Voice of Freedom* program from Corregidor, but in the evening we picked up Tokyo by short wave. There were profuse apologies for the bombing. It was "accidental" and it wouldn't happen again. The Japanese prisoners were positive it was a mistake. They said that all pilots, before they left Japan, were instructed not to fly over hospitals, much less bomb them.

We really believed it must have been a mistake; you get used to thinking the Red

Cross sign marks a sanctuary, inviolable even by the vilest enemy. Nevertheless, additional red crosses were strewn over the grounds, and we rigged up a siren in a tree with a guard posted by it.

Nightmares in the wards were more prevalent than ever after this. A voice would shout, "Hit the floor, hit the floor! Bombers overhead!" Startled half-awake, some of the patients would actually roll to the floor, and even the nurses were sometimes caught off-guard and would flop obediently.

Then someone would growl, "What the hell goes on? Can't a guy sleep around here?"

"Bombers . . . Hit the floor, boys," and the nurse, somewhat embarrassed, would try to wake him up, when often another dreamer down the ward would rip out more advice about falling into fox holes, or yell, "Watch that bastard, he's coming over!"

The possibilities of a gas attack, though they never materialized, were now ever present in our minds and each of us kept gas mask and helmet close at hand. Hogan was especially worried about her mask, which she was sure did not contain the necessary amount of oxygen.

"No wonder," I told her, "the way you used it those first days in Manila."

When we had our first air-raid alarm at Sternberg, I had dashed to Hogan's room expecting to find her there, but she was gone. Then I hurried to the porch of the Nurses' Quarters and saw her spread out on the ground. The fox holes had not yet been dug. Hogan was wearing her gas mask, and the tube leading into the oxygen compartment was pumping away at a great rate. I had not heard any general gas alarm, but she was playing safe.

Now, in Little Baguio, there were no extra gas masks to be distributed. Hogan decided to take the mask of one of the patients who had died.

"How do you know it's any better than yours?" I asked her.

"Well," she retorted, "I'm sure he wasn't as big a damn fool as I was."

One day several doctors and nurses were sitting around trying to relax—and sitting, I might add, on the Red Cross sheets stretched on the ground, for we found ourselves remaining close to that insignia of safety on our off-duty hours—when suddenly the ground shook beneath us. We scrambled to our feet and found that we couldn't stand. Then it stopped as abruptly as it began.

One of the doctors pointed to some cracks in the ground.

"Earthquake," he said, laconically.

It was anti-climactic and yet rather terrifying.

The chief nurse called us in to tell us that our food supply was practically gone. With the bombers overhead constantly now, it was impossible to get anything through to us. Soon there would be only one meal a day.

"We've got to make what we have last," she said. "If necessary, we'll have one meal every two days. I know you won't complain."

We could take it, but what about the patients? They were weak; how could they live with anything less than they had?

Early one evening when it seemed comparatively quiet I went to Hospital No. 2 to visit the girls there. The hospital was larger than ours, spread out and not requiring the stacking of beds one on top of the other. I noticed in one ward that fox holes were dug under the beds and it seemed a practical idea to me.

The doctors and nurses at No. 2 were also working extremely hard. Each had a great number of patients in his or her care, but most of them seemed to be holding up remarkably well.

Their camp, though roomier, was cruder than ours. The Nurses' Quarters consisted of half-shelters strung through the trees, and while we at No. 1 had some sort of crude shower arrangement in our quarters, the girls at No. 2 did their bathing and laundry in a creek. I went down there with several of them, sitting on a rock, talking with them. Most of the girls were dressed in clothes similar to ours: large coveralls, or G.I. Army trousers and shirts, G.I. shoes.

It was fun. We sang songs and talked about old times at Sternberg and Stotsenburg, and went into meticulous detail about the Easter outfits we'd had, and discussed the B.B.B. club that was in the making. Male members were to be known as the Battling Bastards of Bataan; female members, Battling Belles of Bataan.

There were great plans for future reunions at San Francisco or New York.

Even our talk about convoys had stopped. What was the use? The Japanese had the Islands sewed up; we could only hang on and do our jobs.

The Japs were making good their threat to General Wainwright. Near-by targets were bombed continuously. You could smell battle in the air, the heavy smoke and burnt powder; there was the constant noise in your ears, day and night. Over the *Voice of Freedom* station came words of praise from the States.

"You can't shoot with 'em," one of the patients said grimly. But they were good words.

The men in the wards were different, more silent, harder and thoughtful. The shell-shocked cases suffered from the noise of the bombings. At the sound of a close one, some of them hid under their beds and screamed. They trembled violently even at the sound of a truck-motor. Sometimes the younger boys turned to us for comfort.

"What'll happen to us if help doesn't get here?"

We tried, but whatever we could say hadn't much comfort in it.

None of the men boasted of their bravery. No one said he was not frightened. You can't be under or close to constant bombing for days and feel no fear. There was plenty of courage; but no bravado.

I thought a lot about my family during that time. Mother has the "green touch"; her garden at home in the little South Carolina town of Swansea was always lovely, trim and weeded and brimming over with flowers through every season, very different from the ragged lush jungle that surrounded me. We had had a fine childhood, my sisters and my two brothers and myself. It was my idolization of my elder sister that first made me think of being a nurse. Then, after I had trained at the State Hospital, my desire to travel got the better of me, and (through some train of reasoning I can't now follow) I took a business course. Of course I soon found that commercial jobs were not an Open Sesame to the wide, wide world, and moreover, I sadly missed the human element in nursing. It was then I had applied for the Army Nurse Corps. Join the Army and See the World. . . .

When my transfer to the Philippines came through, General Pershing was a patient at the Army and Navy Hospital in Hot Springs, where I was on duty. He told me some of his experiences in the Islands and warned me about the sticky climate and the contaminated garden truck that I mustn't eat. I had great plans. One thing—I was surely going to see Japan. It wasn't so far from the Philippines, and I would go there on one of my vacations—preferably when the cherry trees were in blossom.

My trip to Japan had never materialized, but the Japanese had come to me, and not bearing cherry blossoms nor an olive branch.

On Easter Sunday most of us managed, though we were very busy, to slip away to attend services at one or the other of our chapels. Easter should be a season of hope, but to us on Bataan, it was not that. It was a time of waiting for a greater terror than we had yet known.

VI

At ten o'clock on Easter Monday the first wave of bombers struck us.

Someone yelled, "Planes overhead!" But those had become such familiar words that most of us paid them little attention. I went on pouring medications, and then the drone of the planes was lost in the shrill crescendo and roar of a crashing bomb.

It landed at the hospital entrance and blew up an ammunition truck that was passing. The concussion threw me to the floor. There was a spattering of shrapnel and pebbles and earth on the tin roof. Then silence for a few minutes.

I heard the corpsmen rushing out with litters, and I pulled myself to my feet. Precious medicines were dripping to the ground from the shattered dressing carts, and I tried to salvage as much as possible.

The first casualties came in. The boys in the ammunition truck had been killed, but the two guards at the hospital gate had jumped into their fox holes. By the time they were extricated from the débris that filled up the holes they were both shell-shock cases.

There were plenty of others.

Outside the shed a guard yelled, "They're coming back!"

They were after us, all right.

In the Orthopedic ward nurses and corpsmen began to cut the traction ropes so that the patients could roll out of bed if necessary, broken bones and all. In my ward several of the men became hysterical; I would have joined them if I could. It was all I could do to go on being calm and acting as if everything were all right and I had everything under control.

"They're very near us!" came the warning from outside.

Father Cummins had come in, and standing in the middle of the shed where all the boys could see him, he asked us to repeat the Lord's Prayer with him.

Then the second wave of bombs fell.

That one hit the mess and the Doctors' and Nurses' Quarters. When the ripping and tearing sound of crashing wood and the roar of minor explosions diminished, I could hear shrieks of pain outside, the helpless sobbing of the men in the wards, and Father Cummins' quiet voice praying.

Through the open sides of the sheds came flying débris, clouds of dust, wrenched boards with protruding nails, limbs of trees.

It wasn't over.

Even in the first few moments of quiet, we heard the planes coming back.

We couldn't do anything but wait. That was the awful part; we couldn't do anything.

This time they scored a direct hit on the wards. A thousand-pound bomb pulverized the bamboo sheds, smashed the tin roofs into flying pieces; the iron beds doubled and broke jaggedly like paper matches. Sergeant May had pulled me under a desk, but the desk was blown into the air, he and I with it.

I heard myself gasping. My eyes were being gouged out of their sockets, my whole body was swollen and torn apart by the violent pressure. This is the end, I thought.

Then I fell back to the floor, the desk landing on top of me and bouncing around drunkenly. Sergeant May knocked it away from me, and gasping for breath, bruised and aching, sick from swallowing the smoke of the explosive, I dragged myself to my feet. I heard Freeman, our boy with no legs, calling out:

"Where's Miss Redmond? Is Miss Redmond alive?"

He was being carried out; fortunately, he had rolled out of bed and, though he had been covered with débris, except for a few scratches he was unhurt.

Father Cummins said calmly: "Somebody take over. I'm wounded." He had shrapnel in his shoulder.

Only one small section of my ward remained standing. Part of the roof had been blown into the jungle. There were mangled bodies under the ruins; a blood-stained hand stuck up through a pile of scrap; arms and legs had been ripped off and flung among the rubbish. Some of the mangled torsos were almost impossible to identify. One of the few corpsmen who had survived unhurt climbed a tree to bring down a body blown into the top branches. Blankets, mattresses, pajama tops hung in the shattered trees.

We worked wildly to get to the men who might be buried, still alive, under the mass of wreckage, tearing apart the smashed beds to reach the wounded and the dead. These men were our patients, our responsibility; I think we were all tortured by an instinctive, irrational feeling that we had failed them.

The bombing had stopped, but the air was rent by the awful screams of the new-wounded and the dying, trees were still crashing in the jungle and when one near by fell on the remaining segment of tin roof it sounded like shellfire. We were shaking and sick at our stomachs, but none of us who was able to go on dared to stop even for a moment.

I saw Rosemary Hogan being helped from her ward. Blood streamed from her face and her shoulder; she looked ghastly.

"Hogan," I called, "Hogan, is it bad?"

She managed to wave her good arm at me. "Just a little nose bleed," she said cheerfully.

That was Hogan, all right. "How about you?"

"I'm okay."

The corpsmen led her off to Surgery, which luckily was still standing.

Then Rita Palmer was taken from her ward. Her face and arms had been cut and her skirt and G.I. shirt had been blown off.

I asked a doctor about the other nurses.

"They're all safe," he said.

But there was no time for thankfulness; we were driven by a terrible urgency to save the twice-wounded patients who were still living; to save the medical aids that would keep them alive.

Kitchen utensils from the destroyed mess were strewn over the grounds. From the shattered Receiving ward case records blew about like confetti. The pharmacy had been hit and most of the drugs were gone, but some cabinets were found to be not too badly smashed and there was a swift desperate search for bottles and boxes that could be salvaged.

Someone yelled that the bombers were coming back, but most of us were simply too battered and too tired to react one way or the other. Some people ran to the fox holes, others just didn't bother.

It was one plane and it circled over us maddeningly: Photo Joe, the Japanese flier who took pictures of struck targets.

On my way to Surgery, I saw blind Eugenio groping his way up the slope.

"Eugenio!" I cried. "Where were you? Are you all right?"

His face brightened, as it always did when we spoke to him. "I'm all right, mum." He said he had rolled out of bed and managed later to pull himself out of the débris. "Please, mum," he said, "where am I now?"

I told him, near the operating room, and he

said self-sufficiently, "Then I guess I can get back to my bed."

"Not yet," I said gently. "You sit down here and rest." Eugenio's bed had been completely wrecked and when we had looked for him we thought he was gone too.

With the doctors, each of the nurses on ward-duty made a survey and a record of the living and the dead from her ward. Several of my boys had died of shock; they hadn't been hit, they had been too weak to live through the explosion.

There had been about sixteen hundred beds, or makeshift beds, in our hospital. Now there were only sixty-five left standing. The near-by camps were sending us help, men and supplies, trucks and busses and other vehicles since most of ours were destroyed, and we transferred most of the patients to Hospital No. 2, keeping only those too badly injured to move. Rosemary

Hogan and Rita Palmer were taken to Corregidor.

Perhaps I am making this sound as if it all took a long time. It didn't; it was all in the same day of the bombing. And the bombers were still strafing us, though never as they had in the morning. We placed as many patients as we dared near, or even in, the fox holes; but there were those whom it was too dangerous to move and we had to leave them in the beds we had cleaned out in the section of the shed still standing.

The corpsmen tried to make the nurses stay near the fox holes, while they cleaned up the grounds and attended to the patients.

"We can run faster than you can," they said.

However, it was impossible to do much work that afternoon. We waited for darkness and then the entire staff pitched in. We gathered together as many records as we could find and sorted out the wreckage for every scrap of material and supplies that could be salvaged. There were holes to avoid and tin roofing that might collapse at any moment and we had to work by flashlight. We still uncovered arms and legs and mutilated bodies.

That night there were many burials.

Usually the dead were buried as quickly and quietly and reverently as was possible. A grave registration unit was attached to each hospital which attended to all the details and kept the records. We tried not to disturb the other patients in the wards, but the beds were so close that even by moving the deceased patient at night, someone was bound to hear. Night nurses often found that the patient in the next bed had disappeared, especially if he were a Filipino, and was hiding under some other bed. If he stayed in his own bed, he would explain, he would be the next to die.

But this was wholesale burial. We tried not to hear the scraping of the spades or the thud of earth thrown on earth, but we couldn't get away from it. We couldn't be impersonal or detached.

That night we stayed in our fox holes. I didn't sleep. We hadn't eaten since breakfast, but I wasn't hungry. We were like hunted animals, waiting for the kill, almost hoping it would happen quickly so that the torment of waiting would end. But stronger than that was anger; anger and hate and a hot desire to fight back, to avenge our dead.

What kind of human beings would deliberately bomb a hospital, defenseless, openly marked for what it was, filled with the wounded and the sick?

I don't know. The only answer I had found when I crawled out of my hole in the morning, my head aching, a crick in my back, my legs cramped, was not an answer but a conviction. This isn't a war in which anybody—*anybody*—is let off. Each single individual of us is in it and each must give everything he has to give. An enemy that will bomb hospitals and undefended cities—sick and injured men, or women and children and helpless old people—isn't an enemy you can ever come to terms with; not in the usual meaning of the phrase. The war must end without compromise.

It wasn't particularly original thinking, I know, but somehow it comforted me to have it clear and simple in my own mind. I could put the long thoughts of the people I would never see again into the background and go on about my work.

The bombers were aiming at near-by targets all morning, and we gave medications between leaps into the fox holes. I kept running back and forth between my ward and the trench until Alice Zwicker shouted after me:

"Red, for heaven's sake, stop running around out there. They're coming over again. You get back here and put your helmet on."

It was crowded, damp and dark in the fox hole, but I jumped in obediently as the planes circled over us. Zwick kept saying over and over, "Oh, God, send them away. Oh, God, send them away." Finally they flew off, and instantly Zwick jumped up and shook her fist at them.

"You'd better not come back!" she yelled after them, and followed that warning with an angry stream of very fancy swear words. We all shrieked with laughter, and she turned on us furiously.

"What are you laughing at?" she demanded. "I don't see a damn thing that's funny."

"Do you really want to know?" I said.

"I certainly do. It seems to me you have a queer sense of humor."

I explained, "Just a few minutes ago you were praying so earnestly and then you turn around and in the same breath give the Japs unholy what-for in some of the finest cuss-words I ever heard."

She was horrified. "I did no such thing," she said.

"Oh, yes, you did."

"But I *didn't*. . . ."

"Never mind," said one of the girls soothingly. "If I go first I'll put in a good word for you."

We managed to get together some sort of meal that day, and slowly, under great handicaps, the hospital began to function again. The dressing carts were far from complete, but we made out with what we had as best we could. We concocted many substitutes, rather proud of our ingenuity, and set the Filipinos' clever hands to work making others, such as applicators, for instance, which they made out of stems stripped from the branch of a tree, and then whittled and smoothed into shape.

We wouldn't have been surprised to hear

that the hospital site was to be abandoned, but evidently this was not planned, for carpenters were soon busy tacking oilcloth and black paper over the blasted Surgery windows, and we heard that engineers were to be sent out to help us re-establish the hospital.

But that evening of April 7th at six o'clock heavy artillery shells burst through the jungles around our base. Still unknown to us, Bataan was falling. Fort Drum, Fort Hughes, and Corregidor were firing on Bataan beyond our retreating troops, trying to hold back the Japanese forces.

A little over an hour later, the nurses were ordered to be ready to leave in fifteen minutes. There was a bus provided for us, and Captain Nelson would drive down with us to the docks where we would embark for Corregidor.

There was too much to be done and said in so little time. We wanted to discuss certain details about our patients; we wanted to leave careful instructions for the care of those we were particularly worried about; we wanted to know what was happening, why we were being ordered out. . . .

It hurt to say goodbye. All the doctors and corpsmen were there to see us off, and some of them kept saying it wasn't goodbye; in a few days we'd be back again, but nobody believed them. They said it had been good working with us. They said we'd been brave soldiers.

"We'll be seeing you," they all repeated firmly.

VII

WE HAD NOT BEEN LONG OUT OF sight of the hospital when Captain Nelson held up his hand for attention.

"Girls, there are going to be a lot of trucks, soldiers, civilians on the road. There'll be a great deal of confusion, and I'm asking you to be just as quiet as you can." His voice changed. "Bataan has fallen," he said gravely.

It shocked us into silence. But now that it had happened, we realized how we had been hiding from the thought, refusing to believe it could happen this way, in spite of the bombings, the strafing, the stories the soldiers brought in from the field. We couldn't honestly be surprised that it had come at last.

Only . . . what about the others? The doctors and corpsmen we had just left, the patients, the chaplains? What about the people at Hospital No. 2 and our little Bataana and her mother, off in the jungle somewhere, *would they get out in time?*

We didn't say any of these things out loud; we didn't need to, each of us knew what the others were thinking.

The road was bumpy and we bucked and jolted along slowly, traveling without lights. Occasionally one of the trucks switched on a light and the guards posted along the way cursed loudly.

"Tryin' to signal the —— bastards? Douse it, douse it, you damn fool. . . ."

It was bad driving, for the road was heavy with traffic of all sorts. Streams of trucks and tanks rumbled ahead of us. Troops marched quickly along the side of the road, and civilians fleeing from their homes wove frantically between the cars trying to hurry, unnerving the drivers. They banged on the sides of the bus, pleading with us to take them, to carry them away before the Japanese caught them. It was horrible to catch glimpses through the dark of their panic-stricken faces, to hear them crying out to us over the roar of motors and the tramp of marching feet, and to know there was nothing we could do for them.

Every now and then Captain Nelson would say quietly, "Take it easy, girls, take it easy. I'm sorry for them too, but we can't take them all and it's that or nothing."

We reached the docks finally, to find them crowded with incessant activity; soldiers were massing for embarkation, trucks kept rolling in, officers ran here and there through the darkness snapping out orders. We could hear the water lapping at the piles, and boats pulling away.

Colonel Carpenter, in charge of the evacuation, told us we would have to wait, there were others scheduled to go over ahead of us. He was worried about an infantry unit that had failed to arrive as planned, and which should have been sent to Corregidor some time ago.

"But what about the girls at No. 2?" we insisted. "What will they do?"

"They've been ordered out also," he told us over his shoulder.

Bombers came over while we waited, unloading on targets not far away. We were told to run to the fox holes, but as we didn't know where they were, we stayed on the dock. Some of the girls were so exhausted that they fell asleep stretched out on the wooden boards. The rest of us huddled together, watching the shells landing on Corregidor and streaks of flame leaping against the black sky. The bay seemed alive with shadowy forms of boats and native rafts, plying back and forth. Several were struck by artillery fire. Sick at heart we watched them sink and listened to the cries of the drowning grow faint and finally die away.

At twelve o'clock our turn came. We scuttled into the boat that was waiting for us; it was small and open and, like all the others, unarmed.

I looked back to watch the burning shores of Bataan. The boat reverberated from the blasts as ammunition dumps were destroyed, and often a piece of wreckage blown through the air would bang on her sides. Smoke rolled up from gasoline drums that had been saved for the planes that never came.

About halfway over we found ourselves under cross-fire from Corregidor and the enemy lines on Bataan.

We made port at Corregidor at half past three that morning: a trip that usually took three quarters of an hour had taken us three hours and a half.

We were rushed through the Malinta Tunnel into the heart of the huge rock. Corregidor seemed impregnable, another Gibraltar, witl its vast intricate network of tunnels. It wa good to be there, to be greeted by friends, an given hot food and beds; to feel safe again.

Next day at noon the girls from Hospita No. 2 joined us. Their experience had bee horrible. They had been ordered to leave fro the Cabcaben docks, which were the nearest t their base, but on the way they learned that th docks had already been taken by the Japanese Loaded in garbage trucks they tried to reacl Mariveles, but wrecked cars, army and civilia traffic, and a destroyed ammunition dump kep them hours on the road. As, finally, the reached the waterfront, they saw the last inter island boat steam away. It had been held fo them a long time, and when all hope of thei arrival was gone, another group had been take across in their place. By this time Bataan ha surrendered, but fortunately the Japanese ha not yet reached the wharves.

The girls were frantic. In desperation, a few managed to find places on barges and rough tugs that were attempting the crossing, but the majority were stranded on the docks, until at last a boat was sent out from Corregidor, and when they reached the Tunnel they found the other girls waiting for them.

Two of the A.N.C. nurses were missing. They had been cut off at Baguio, the resort city, fairly early in the war, and we heard that they and the officers of their small hospital base had escaped to the hills and joined in guerrilla warfare; that was the last report we had of them.

With the surrender of Bataan, numbers of escaped soldiers made their way to Corregidor. Somehow they got to the waterfront, somehow they swam until a boat picked them up, or they found some small leaking forgotten raft and made their way across the water. Many tried and failed. Some were drowned, others were picked off by snipers. Captain Marvin Tanahill was brought in so exhausted that he could not tell us for several days how he had escaped. He had marched up with his men and surrendered, as ordered. His clothing and firearms had been taken away from him, and in his underwear he stood in the line of American prisoners. Suddenly he felt he couldn't stand it; he would rather die. So he turned and began to walk away, fully expecting to be shot in the back. Nothing happened. He passed the Japanese guards and still nothing happened. He went on, marveling at every step that he was alive, until he found himself at the shore. He began to swim across the bay and at last was rescued by a barge.

There was little comfort to be found in looking ahead, for though our underground fortress might be impregnable, supplying it was less than ever possible. If aid could not reach us while Bataan still held, we all knew (though the words were seldom spoken) that no relief could be hoped for now.

But there was true comfort and a quickening of pride and faith in the words that went from General Wainwright's Headquarters to the people at home:

"Bataan has fallen. The Philippine American troops on this war-ravaged and bloodstained peninsula have laid down their arms—with heads bloody but unbowed they have yielded to superior force and numbers of the enemy. The world will long remember the epic struggle that Filipino and American soldiers put up in the jungle fortresses and along the rugged coast of Bataan. They have stood up uncomplaining under the constant and grueling fire of the enemy for more than three months. Besieged on land and blockaded by sea, cut off from all help in the Philippine Islands and America, these intrepid fighters have borne all that human endurance could bear.

"For what sustained them through all their months of incessant battle was a force that was more than merely physical. It was the force of an unconquerable faith, something in the heart and soul that physical hardships and adversity could not destroy. It was the thought of their native land and all that it holds most dear, the thought of freedom, dignity and pride, in these, most priceless of all, our human prerogatives. The adversary, in the pride of his power and triumph, will credit our troops with nothing less than the courage and fortitude that his own troops have shown in battle. Our men have fought a brave and bitterly contested struggle, all the world will testify to the almost superhuman endurance with which they stood up until the last in the face of overwhelming odds.

"But the decision had to come. Men fighting under a banner of unshakable faith are made of something more than flesh, but they are not made of impervious steel. The flesh must yield at last, endurance melts away and the end of battle must come.

"Bataan has fallen, but the spirit that made it stand—a beacon to all the liberty-loving peoples of the world—cannot fall."

VIII

THERE WERE TOO MANY PATIENTS to allow the nurses from Bataan to rest very long, and soon we were assigned to various Hospital Tunnels. By that time I had learned more about the labyrinth that is the Fortress of Corregidor. The Malinta Tunnel, the main one, ran east and west; stemming from it, north and south, were twenty laterals or smaller tunnels, all of which were numbered, odd on the left, even on the right. Branching from these twenty tunnels were four or five others, running in the same direction as the Malinta. Each lateral housed a special division of the fort—General Wainwright's Headquarters, machine shops, refrigeration plants, Nurses' Quarters, Doctors' Quarters, mess halls, hospital, and so on.

I was in the surgical division and marveled to find it so well equipped; after the crudities of Limay and Hospital No. 2, I couldn't get over the wonder of white enameled tables beside each bed. They seemed almost indecently luxurious.

The men were better nourished than our boys had been, though there wasn't an overabundant or very varied food supply, and there was no malaria on Corregidor except among the boys brought over from Bataan.

We couldn't realize that we dared use electric lights, that there wasn't a blackout. "Solid rock overhead," we had to tell ourselves again and again.

We had two white sheets on each bed. We had enough food to satisfy us. More wonderful than all else was Felicidad, who officially cleaned the Nurses' Quarters, but having saved a supply of soap and nail polish she carried on a flourishing business on the side, specializing in giving shampoos and fingerwaves. She charged seventy-five centavos (about thirty-eight cents) for a manicure and two pesos (one dollar) for a shampoo. Or she said, "You give me what you want," which meant more than her established price.

Felicidad carried on still another business. She bunked with us, and when most of the Bataan nurses had assembled in the Nurses' lateral she pulled out a box from under her bed and conducted a rummage sale. The box was crammed with dresses and other apparel that the Corregidor nurses had given her before the war.

"All right," she would say, holding up a dress before some girl, "this look good on you. How much you give me?"

The rummage sale was a wild scramble, for it had been a long time since we last saw civilian clothes and, moreover, our coveralls and G.I. trousers were very badly worn. We were ready to offer Felicidad anything we had for the clothing she offered for sale, and many of us assembled quite decent costumes—though we had very little opportunity to wear them.

She had a good generous streak in her behind all this shrewdness. Often belts or scarfs were tossed to us, with the off-handed remark that it would look well with such and such a dress; or she might decide that a certain dress would be especially becoming to a particular girl and would refuse to take any payment for it.

Felicidad was terribly worried about her people. There were days when her usually pleasant face was haggard and she would show no interest in anybody or anything. "They are murdering them out there," she muttered unhappily, "and soon they will come for us. How long you think it will be before the Japs really get us?"

She didn't expect an answer. She knew as

well as most that it was only a question of time.

An especially fine Chinese tailor had also taken refuge in the Tunnel, and we could hear his sewing-machine going at top speed behind our lateral, where he was stationed. Eddy was also assigned to cleaning, but he spent his free time sewing for the Quartermaster and anyone else who could engage him. He altered the clothes we purchased from Felicidad, making them fit nicely. Also, some of the officers who had been stationed on Corregidor before the invasion gave the nurses their white sharkskin suits they had managed to save; we tried to hire Eddy to make something from them that we could wear. But he was much too busy and tired. I ripped the trousers, hoping to fashion a skirt from the material myself, but under the pressure of coming events I never found time to finish it.

However, there were several other Chinese tailors who had taken refuge in the Tunnel;

the Quartermaster had them make us really streamlined coveralls, a good-looking skirt and two blouses apiece.

Though it seemed almost sacrilege to find any fault with the place that had given us sanctuary, living underground had certain discomforts. The roar of shells and bombs was not so muffled as I had thought at first, but echoed and reverberated through the laterals; and the lack of real ventilation was hard on everyone, for even the elaborate system of fans did not keep the air from getting very stuffy and hot. And as the shelling of Corregidor became heavier and the bombings more frequent, our luxuries disappeared one by one. Double-decked and triple-decked beds in the hospital; civilian refugees sleeping in packed rows on the Tunnel floors; two meals a day, again, and scanty rations . . . dreadful, familiar and unmistakable signs that the end was drawing near.

Apparently the Japanese were not aiming directly at the Tunnel, as yet; they blasted the field units and other military objectives, refrigeration plants, warehouses; sometimes there would not be a man left out of an entire unit. For the men outside there was no escape from the constant shelling, except for their improvised tunnels and fox holes. At this time there was frequent admission of severe shell-shock cases. Men stationed close enough to the Tunnel came inside after being relieved from duty. Officers and privates alike dropped into the sleep of utter exhaustion wherever they could find a place to lie down, and in their bloodshot, weary eyes was the look we had come to know during those last days on Bataan.

In a way the civilian refugees wrenched at our hearts more than the soldiers. There were new ones every day; frightened, exhausted, hungry, their homes and often their families destroyed, helpless and without hope; all they asked was shelter from the hell outside. One of the most heartbreaking cases was six-year-old Fernandez. On the evening Bataan fell he had been found wandering along the docks, crying. His family had all been killed, and some soldiers picked him up and brought him with them to Corregidor. On his arrival at the Tunnel it was found that he had a severe case of malaria and was running a temperature of 104 degrees. As he improved the question arose as to what should be done with him. Some of the Filipino soldiers wanted to adopt him, but it was of course unsafe to take him out of the Tunnel into the field camps.

Fernandez had a way of staring at you very gravely and then his eyes would gradually brighten in a glow of affection. A corner of one of the laterals was cleared and a bed improvised for him in an old bathtub. Eddy, the Chinese tailor, made several suits for him and he was generally petted and made much of, with most of us taking a hand at teaching him English and manners according to American standards.

When he came to my desk one day I told him he must say, "Good morning." He ran away again, and reappeared several hours later.

"Good morning, Miss Redmond," he said brightly.

"No, Fernandez," I said, "you must say 'good afternoon.' "

He stood still, blinking his eyes at me, very much puzzled and hurt, until I put my arms around him and explained.

General Wainwright issued an order that every able person in the Tunnel must work, without exception, which not only relieved the overworked hospital staff of a good many details, but was undoubtedly excellent for the general morale. Considering the almost intolerable strain under which every person on Corregidor was living, there was extraordinarily little hysteria or complaining, and the General's own unfailing cheerfulness, the atmosphere of courage and friendliness he brought with him when he made his rounds, set the example for each of us. Army people and civilians alike tried their best to follow.

We did have a case of hysteria in the hospital, one so serious as to border on insanity. The boy had been standing at a battery gun talking to a friend. There was shelling going on around them though they seemed to be out of the direct line of fire. Our patient dropped something and bent down to retrieve it, going on with his conversation. As he straightened up, the shell-torn head of his friend flew past his face and the shattered body fell at his feet.

There was one case of infantile paralysis. It was not epidemic; Ted's was the only case, and we never learned where he had contracted it. We kept him isolated as much as possible from the other patients, and though his legs were paralyzed he seemed to be improving. Ted was always cheerful. He talked about returning to the States and going to Warm Springs. Look at President Roosevelt, he said confidently, there was a swell proof that polio could be cured. He hoped he wouldn't have to wear braces too long; he was a jitterbug, he confided, and this illness surely would cramp his style. One evening he became suddenly worse, and in spite of everything we could do for him, he died.

At one time we had two hundred cases of food poisoning, an entire battery division. They had eaten contaminated meat and they were a very sick bunch of boys. In the overcrowded and stuffy Tunnel that particular ailment was especially unpleasant, complicated by a shortage of emesis pans, for which we had to substitute pails and bowls and buckets, and by the fact that we had to put the boys in double rows of double-decked beds. However, they were soon well again, rather weak but otherwise none the worse for the experience.

In the evenings both soldiers and civilians living in the Tunnel had a habit of going outside, near the gates, for a breath of fresh air. Of course we had an air-warning system; if a bomber was sighted, red lights would flash inside the Tunnel signaling that no one was to leave, and outside, sirens blew, warning those who had left the Tunnel to return.

I had been on Corregidor for two weeks when one of these nightly airings ended in disaster. Someone in the crowd noticed a flare going up overhead and tried to shout an alarm, but it was too late. A shell exploded near the entrance. There was a panic-stricken rush for the gate, but the concussion had closed it and it could not be opened from the outside. Another shell landed in the crowd.

Inside, we had heard the screaming of the shells. All the doctors and nurses hurried to duty, as the gates were opened and corpsmen ran out with stretchers to bring in the wounded.

The shells had done their work well.

We worked all that night, and I wish I could forget those endless, harrowing hours. Hours of giving injections, anesthetizing, ripping off clothes, stitching gaping wounds, of amputations, sterilizing instruments, bandaging, settling the treated patients in their beds, covering the wounded that we could not save. . . .

I had still not grown accustomed to seeing people torn and bleeding and dying in numbers like these. When *one* patient dies it is agonizing enough; when you are faced by such mass suffering and death something cracks inside you, you can't ever be quite the same again.

Only while it's happening, there's a sort of blessed numbness that keeps you going, keeps you making the right motions, finding the right things to do.

That night some died before we could get to them. Legs and arms had been wrenched off;

there were jagged flesh wounds; pieces of exploded shrapnel stuck in ugly wounds; deaths from shock mounted no matter how frantically we worked over the victims.

One boy, half-conscious, his leg hanging by shreds from his thigh, said to me through gritted teeth, "Don't cut off . . . my clothes . . . got no underpants on. . . ."

The litter-bearers kept bringing in more and more. Once, as I stooped to give an injection to one that they had just put down on the floor, I saw that it was a headless body. Shock and horror made me turn furiously on the corpsmen.

"*Must* you do this?" I cried.

The boys looked at what they had carried with consternation almost equaling mine.

"It's so dark out there," one of them stammered. "We can't use lights. We feel for the bodies and just roll them onto the stretchers."

The doctors were so busy with the more severe cases that they turned minor injuries over to the nurses. "You take this one," they would say, going on down the long line. And, "You can handle that."

I was ordered to take care of a patient whose great toe was badly cut by shrapnel. I asked the doctor:

"What shall I do?"

"Remove it. It's practically off now; you won't have to do much to finish the job."

When I dropped the toe from my instrument into the container in which we disposed of the amputated parts, it fell into the open hand of an arm that had just been removed.

April 29th was Hirohito's birthday and the Japanese Army, we heard, had promised their Emperor the Philippines as a birthday present.

The week after the accident at the Tunnel gate was marked by a steady worsening of conditions—more casualties from the outside all the time, and our food supplies coming to an end. There was no retreat from Corregidor. We were making our last stand, and we knew it. There was a tendency to talk a great deal about our families and the towns we came from and our childhood. The men we had left on Bataan were always in our minds, and sometimes we wondered about them aloud, but in the big "ifs" of their future ("*If* they get out . . . *If* they're alive"). Now we silently included ourselves.

They began to celebrate the Emperor's birthday at seven-thirty that morning. To my knowledge, we had fourteen air-raid alarms that day. They shelled the three entrances to the Malinta Tunnel; they came at us from all sides.

The whole island was under attack. Topside, Middleside, and Bottomside were pounded without let-up. Once I looked quickly from the entrance, and saw total devastation. Trees were down, the roads were almost hidden under débris, and there were great gaping craters in the earth. The air was heavy with dust and ground particles of wreckage swirling around in gradually diminishing arcs. Under the heavy barrage it was impossible to bring the wounded into the Tunnel, and medical help was sent outside.

In the Tunnel we were jarred by the force of the explosions. Bottles, dishes, any loose objects, were flung from tables and shelves and often both men and women near the Tunnel entrances were sent sprawling to the floor. Smoke filled the laterals, filling our eyes with tears and making breathing difficult. But still we had the security of that solid rock overhead; it was better than waiting in a fox hole.

At six o'clock I received word from the Chief Nurse, Captain Maud Davison, to report at the mess hall. Twenty-two nurses were sent for, each of us surprised at the summons, and each of us I think torn, as I was, between joy and sorrow when we heard that we were relieved of our assignment in Corregidor.

We were to leave at half-past nine that evening; we were not to say goodbye to anyone nor discuss our departure. Each would be permitted to carry a muzette bag which must not weigh more than ten pounds when packed. Two planes would carry us to Melbourne, Australia, where we were ordered to report for further instructions.

I did not know what to think, nor how I felt. I wanted to go, and I didn't want to go. Probably I would never see the other nurses again, and I wanted to stay with them and face whatever was to come; we had faced so much together, I felt like a deserter.

Then there were the others—the doctors, the corpsmen, the officers and privates, the patients, the Filipino civilians of whom I had grown fond, like Felicidad and little Fernandez. It was like leaving Bataan all over again, only sharper this time. For I was leaving the Islands, I was leaving a losing battle—a lost battle.

Not that I hadn't, along with everyone else, entertained dreams of escape; not that my instinct for self-preservation wasn't as strong as anybody's. I don't think I had any illusions about what the end would be like, waiting in a bomb-target for the finish, watching destroyed men die, seeing the food supply get lower and lower and the signs of hunger etched in my friends' faces, feeling myself the pangs of near-starvation, and as the medical supplies dwindled, concocting substitutes that were no substitutes for healing sick and wounded men. . . .

The odds were against our getting to Australia, but as an officer in the U. S. Army I was to obey orders. . . .

In spite of precautions, word had spread through the Tunnel that we were leaving. People were waiting at the entrance to whisper goodbye.

It was a strangely quiet night. The Japanese apparently thought they had done a good day's work and could afford to celebrate the Emperor's birthday in a more convivial fashion. Our guns held their fire, too.

General Wainwright's car led the small procession as we slowly and cautiously made our way through the wreckage to the docks. Three weeks ago we had escaped from Bataan, and as we waited at the waterfront for the boats that would take us to the planes, I was glad that Hatch and Hogan were in the group. It was right and fitting; we had been together at Manila and now we were together on the docks of Corregidor—the beginning and the end.

IX

THE PILOTS OF THE PBY'S HURried us into the planes, while we fervently hoped that the Japanese were too befuddled by *sake* to notice the ships that skimmed the surface of the water like huge dragonflies. Hogan went in the first plane, Hatch and I in the other.

The pilot kept saying, "Let's get going. Hurry up . . . hurry up."

The crew were frankly nervous; they had volunteered for this assignment which had been presented to them in Australia as a suicide mission. But we took off smoothly from the silvery waters of the bay, with a last view of the burning shore lines of Bataan and Corregidor as we gained altitude. The two steel bars running along the body of the plane, which constituted the seating arrangements, were crowded and I went to the rear and sat there with the gun crew.

Looking down, I saw the other plane flying below us, then it shot ahead and was soon out of sight. Far below rings of smoke hovered in the air and little balls of fire flashed through the sky like falling stars.

"What are they?" I asked the man nearest me.

"Well," he said drily, "it could be anti-aircraft, sister."

The air was exhilaratingly fresh after our weeks in the hot stale atmosphere of the Tunnel, but it was also very cold. Most of us were anemic, all of us physically under par, and we shivered unhappily in our coveralls which were all we had with us. The crew found extra coats which we burrowed under like cats under a blanket, and once we were warm we felt safe and untroubled, leaving whatever worrying might be done to the pilots and the crew.

Before we reached Lake Lanao, next morning, we ran into a heavy fog which forced us down, and the plane taxied around in the water for about thirty minutes, surrounded by vapor so heavy that we couldn't see a foot beyond the windows.

"At least the Japs can't spot us in this," one of the crew remarked genially. "Packed in cotton wool. Good as a smokescreen."

Then the fog lifted and we went on to Lake Lanao, in the northern part of Mindanao, one of the southernmost islands of the Philippines. We were taken to a small Army encampment where we met the girls from the other plane, and the soldiers shared with us their breakfast of coconuts, bananas, hot cakes, and weak coffee.

The Japanese had successfully made a landing on the Island of Mindanao this very morning; they were only forty miles away. We were to go on to the chief Army base of the island to pick up a few more passengers, and on the way we had to leap out of the bus and take refuge in the rice-paddies while Jap planes roared overhead. I think most of us, at that point, had a feeling that we were being personally hunted down and persecuted; we were too nervously exhausted to have much sense of proportion left.

When we reached the base, we were given another breakfast at the Army and Navy Club. They served us *eggs* . . . we had forgotten what they tasted like. There was toast, too, and good, strong coffee.

The camp was a hive of activity, for preparations were under way for the coming battle, but even so the officers snatched time to come and see us; some of them were old friends from Manila. They got out champagne to celebrate, and we drank to the blithe days before the war, and to the future, and to our friends who were . . . we didn't know where.

When we returned to the village where the planes lay well-camouflaged in a cove, we were told we would have to discard some of the things in our muzette bags to provide for the added weight of the officers who were joining us. We didn't have much to discard, but we dutifully went through our possessions; we all took off our canteens and a few of the air corps men removed their pistols and holsters.

Some of the soldiers who were watching came up at this time and asked if they could have them. They were told that the equipment would be turned over to the Quartermaster.

"There's a helluva long line at the depot all the time," one boy said, "and not enough to go 'round."

Another added, "Not all of us have canteens," and a third chimed in, "I'm posted as guard at the ammunition dump, but I don't have a gun, let alone a pistol. I wouldn't have a chance against those damn snipers."

Whether it was as bad as it sounded, I don't know (soldiers have been known to go to considerable lengths to get hold of a coveted possession) but anyway, the canteens and the pistols changed hands without further discussion.

The boats came and the girls for the first plane piled in.

"So long," they called, "see you tomorrow."

But they were wrong.

The weight in our plane was still too much. Under the pilot's unrelenting eye we threw out more and more of our few remaining possessions. But when the plane still did not rise, we would have gladly thrown everything away. We sat still and tense, willing that plane to rise, to take us away, sick with the thought that if we were going to fall into the hands of the Japanese after all why couldn't we have been with the others at Corregidor?

And then, just as utter despair clutched us, the motor seemed to make a tremendous effort —and the plane rose slowly but steadily. It was almost an hour before the real cause of the trouble was found—a young American soldier stowed away in the tail of the ship.

After that the flight to Australia was as smooth and peaceful as if there were no war.

Darwin showed grim evidences of the heavy bombing on the nineteenth. We went through desolate streets to the hospital which had been damaged too, expecting to find the nurses from the first plane waiting for us there. They weren't, but of course there were any number of things that might have delayed the plane; it might have run into heavy fog, or a storm, or got slightly off its course. . . . A little delay like this meant nothing.

And later in the morning the plane did arrive. But not the nurses and other Army personnel. Not Hogan.

No one knew quite what had happened. The plane had made a landing while still in the Islands, and had hit a rock which did some damage. While the crew made repairs the girls were sent to take shelter with an Army unit near by. When the ship was ready to take off again, the group was not to be found. The crew did everything they could but it was all fruitless, and finally they were forced to leave without them.

We told each other they'd be all right. We said, sure they will, they have a whole division to take care of them, you can't down that lot especially Hogan. . . .

I thought of Hogan on Bataan after the bombing, waving her hand at me; "Just a nosebleed," she'd said. . . .

The city of Melbourne stared at us in astonishment. We had nothing but our forlorn-looking coveralls to wear and it was Australia's winter season. We were thin as famine victims, hungry-eyed, and shivering. Restaurants, hotels, and the Port Melbourne Hospital staff were appalled at the quantities of food we wanted. There was no use offering us a choice of, for instance, ice cream or pie and cheese; we demanded both.

Clothes presented a more difficult problem, for clothing was rationed and we had no cards. But we could get our hair shampooed and trimmed in shape again, and the Port Melbourne nurses generously came to our rescue in the matter of wardrobes. It felt odd, and very satisfactory too, to be wearing skirts and shoes that were not G.I.

"You look almost human again," Hatch assured me kindly.

All of us had lost a great deal of weight, as

much as twenty pounds or over, and we weren't feeling very well. Vitamins, liver extracts, tonics and bed-for-several-days were prescribed for the remainder of our stay in Australia.

Other veterans of Bataan came to see us, men who had had hairbreadth escapes and sometimes were even yet unsure of how they had managed to get away—to fight again, of course, not to safety. Those were happy reunions, for all the sad undercurrent of speculation about our friends who were left behind and the things it was better not to talk about, not yet anyway, not while they were still so fresh in our minds.

Word of Corregidor's surrender came on the second evening we were in Melbourne.

We said to each other, "They won't be bombed any more."

We asked, "They'll be all right, won't they?"

But no one knew any more than we did.

We were in Melbourne for only three weeks. One day we were told we would sail in two hours; some of the girls were shopping or not in the hospital quarters and had to be found (one, who had been having a permanent wave, turned up with half her hair frizzy and the other half very straight); and a general alarm was sounded for Miss Florence MacDonald who was out sightseeing but turned up, nonchalant as ever, just before the boat sailed.

On June 11th, our stormy and perilous voyage came to a safe end in San Francisco Bay. It was not a triumphant homecoming, but it was a very thankful one. Standing at the ship's rail watching the lovely shoreline and the tall buildings of the city, we were filled with new strength, new courage and hope; and I thought: Those are the gifts America bestows not only on her own children but on the whole world, I must never forget that no matter what terrible days are still to come.

Our Bataan duty was not over, even yet.

At the Letterman General Hospital in Presidio, we were admitted as patients. The day after our arrival, Colonel McKie in charge of Public Relations, came to us to say that they had been keeping reporters and news reel photographers away from us until we had rested but there were other people waiting who couldn't be put off so readily. Would we, he said, talk to the relatives of the men on Bataan?

It seemed like an unnecessary question, and we told him so. We would, of course, right away.

And then, for days they waylaid us in the halls or on the stairs as we went to Colonel McKie's office which had been turned over to us, and for hour after hour rich and poor, young and old, waited their turn in long lines. Sometimes we could answer their questions in a way to send them home relieved of the worst of their anxiety. More often we could tell them nothing about their own boys and fell back on whatever we knew of the units . . . where they had been when we had last heard, in what actions they had figured, the conditions under which they had lived. Straws of comfort, but how eagerly they were seized! And sometimes we could only say, "He died like a good soldier. . . ."

Many brought us photographs and showed them to us mutely, unable to speak. There were women who fainted, weeping and hysteria, and there was Spartan courage that was almost harder to bear.

We were deluged by telephone calls and stacks of letters from all over the country which, with the help of stenographers supplied by the Red Cross, we did our best to answer immediately.

. . . the boy's mother is so ill from worry that I am writing this in her stead . . .

. . . he was our only son . . .

. . . he enlisted in the Army as soon as he was old enough . . .

. . . my husband and I weren't married very long . . .

. . . we have three children and I don't know what to tell them of their father . . .

There was so little we could say.

In a way it was harder telling those mothers and wives and fathers about their boys, than anything on Bataan or Corregidor. There we were a part of the fight, we had our work to do, we were under orders and a part of a fighting Army.

It's fine to rest for a while, but I am happier on duty. When I have work to do, I can get too tired to lie awake remembering the soldiers, the doctors and nurses and corpsmen who are my friends and who are prisoners of the Japanese. I hope they know we remember them; I hope,

SSOCIATION, INC.

A bus converted for hospital use.

SOCIATION, INC.

A typical Bataan foxhole.

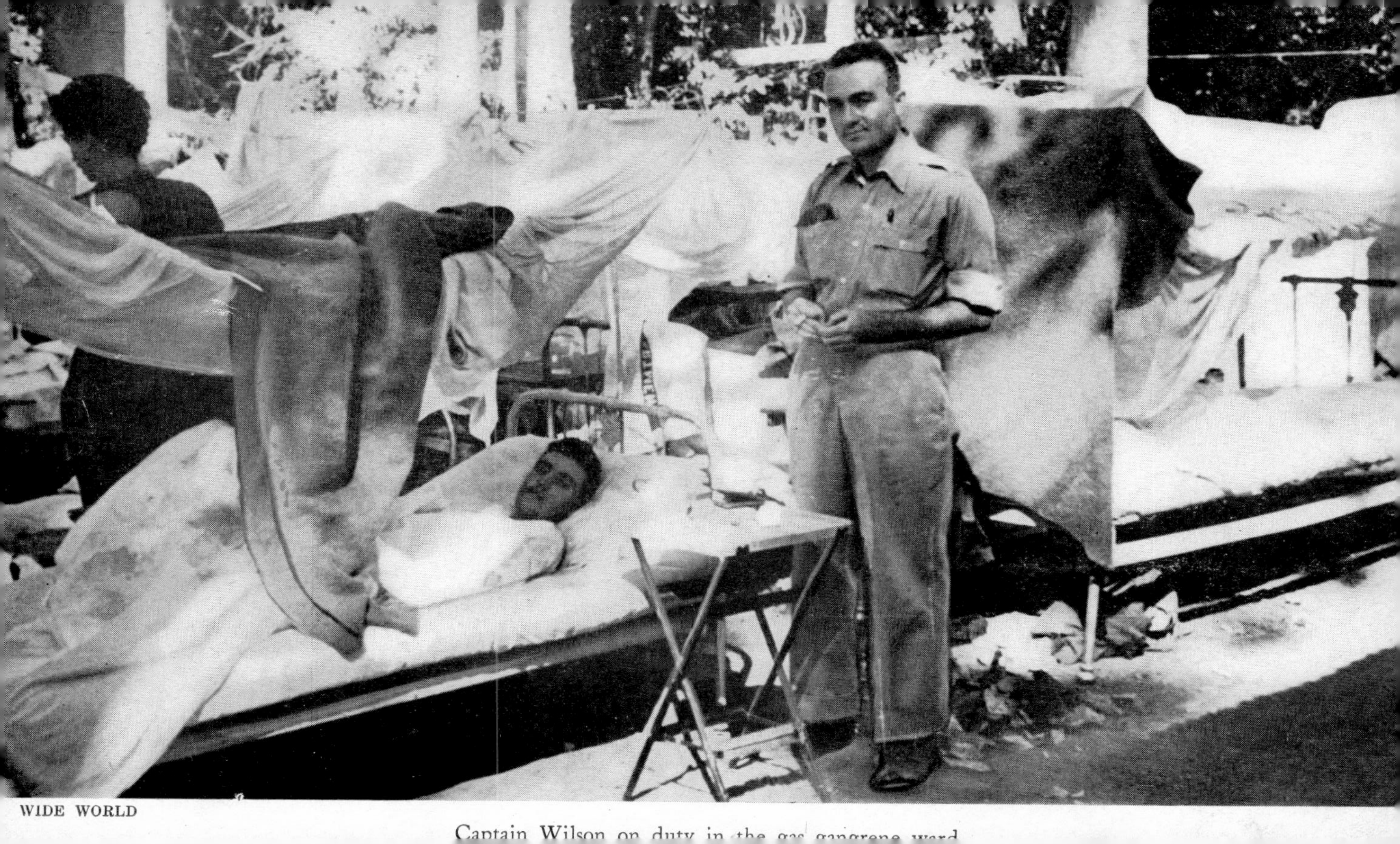

WIDE WORLD

Captain Wilson on duty in the gas gangrene ward

somehow, word gets to them that the offensive they talked about, prayed for, while we waited for help that couldn't reach us, is under way at last.

THE END